Teach us to Pray

EVERETT LEADINGHAM, EDITOR

Though this book is designed for group study, it is also intended for personal enjoyment and spiritual growth. A leader's guide is available from your local bookstore or your publisher.

Be

ISBN: 083-411-965X

Printed in the
United States of America

Editor: Everett Leadingham
Associate Editor: Charlie L. Yourdon
Executive Editor: Randy Cloud
Writers: Ken Bible, Carl Leth, David Nixon, Morris Weigelt

Cover design: Michael Walsh
Cover Photo/Art: Keith Alexander

10 9 8 7 6 5 4 3

Contents

Perhaps one reason God delays His answers to our prayers is because He knows we need to be with Him far more than we need the things we ask of Him.

—Ben Patterson

Psalm 63

[1]O God, you are my God,
   earnestly I seek you;
my soul thirsts for you,
   my body longs for you,
in a dry and weary land
   where there is no water.

[2]I have seen you in the sanctuary
   and beheld your power and your glory.
[3]Because your love is better than life,
   my lips will glorify you.
[4]I will praise you as long as I live,
   and in your name I will lift up my hands.
[5]My soul will be satisfied as with the richest of foods;
   with singing lips my mouth will praise you.

[6]On my bed I remember you;
   I think of you through the watches of the night.
[7]Because you are my help,
   I sing in the shadow of your wings.
[8]My soul clings to you;
   your right hand upholds me.

Psalm 73

[23]Yet I am always with you;
   you hold me by my right hand.
[24]You guide me with your counsel,
   and afterward you will take me into glory.
[25]Whom have I in heaven but you?
   And earth has nothing I desire besides you.
[26]My flesh and my heart may fail,
   but God is the strength of my heart
   and my portion forever.

[27]Those who are far from you will perish;
   you destroy all who are unfaithful to you.
[28]But as for me, it is good to be near God.
   I have made the Sovereign LORD my refuge;
   I will tell of all your deeds.

CHAPTER 1

Prayer Is a Relationship

MOST OF US have lives that are busy, busy, busy. Our schedules are "filled to the gills" even with overlapping appointments. With so many demands upon our time, our attention, and our energies, it is often difficult to focus on and invest quality time in significant relationships: relationships with our family, our relationships within our church, and our relationship with God. Sadly, these significant relationships are treated as if they were fast-food meals. We drive up to the window, place our order, and speed away to that urgent meeting.

A pastor relates this story: "A dear friend of mine who has cancer told me that this was the best thing that had ever happened to him. It stopped him short in the race of life and caused him to reevaluate everything, starting with his relationship with God." Illness and other major events may also bring us to a crisis point, urging us, with new seriousness, to depend upon the Lord. For some it may be a death in the family. For others it may be a major "passage" in life, a conflict in marriage, trouble with children, or a business reversal. These emotional earthquakes will break down our defenses and open us up to the Lord. What we often find then is a deep inner emptiness and a longing for God. Psalms 63 and 73 are a witness to that longing and its satisfaction.

A Love Relationship

Imagine yourself deeply, wholeheartedly in love. Love flows from deep inside you, through every part of your being. That love automatically expresses itself in many ways: in words of love, in expressions of praise and appreciation, in natural joy, in a silent glow of satisfaction. At various moments day and night you think about that one you love so much. You trust this one more and more and want to share every aspect of life with this person.

That is the relationship God wants to have with us. He is an ardent lover, driven by a soul-deep love that never cools off. God described himself to Moses as "the compassionate and gracious God, slow to anger, abounding in love and faithfulness, maintaining love to thousands, and forgiving wickedness, rebellion and sin" (Exodus 34:6-7). He is tender, expressive. He showers us with beautiful words and wonderful gifts. He woos our attention and trust.

Prayer is communication between two who love each other, between God and us. It builds the trust that gradually intertwines our lives wholly with Him. And it has a love-deep effect on us, as it did Moses. "When Moses came down from Mount Sinai with the two tablets of the Testimony in his hands, he was not aware that his face was radiant because he had spoken with the Lord" (Exodus 34:29).

That is what God wants prayer to be. He desires communication with us that is open, deep, and constant. And as we turn to Him, He will work in us to develop the kind of prayer life that makes us glow with the glory of His love.

Prayer Is Reaching Out to God

When my wife and I are talking, she doesn't appreciate it when my mind and heart are preoccupied. If my eyes are looking elsewhere, if I answer her with a grunt or with "Yeah . . . OK," that's not conversation. She's insulted. She wants me to look at her, listen to her, and respond openly and thoughtfully.

God is no different. If my wife can tell when our conversation is a shallow pretense, can't God as well? We miss the depth of conversation that is possible through prayer when our prayer consists of mere words, spoken from obligation or dry routine.

Prayer is when we reach out to God from our hearts. It starts with our need for Him. We are thirsty for Him, as one gets thirsty for water "in a dry and weary land" (Psalm 63:1).

Notice the passionate and intense verbs that are used to describe the psalmist's desire for God in Psalm 63. The psalmist *seeks* for God, *thirsts* and *longs* for Him, and *looks* to see Him. These verbs are not passive. These are passion-filled verbs that indicate an intense desire to meet with God.

David describes his experience of longing for God in verse 1 with the strong physical metaphor of being thirsty in a desert with no sign of water. Physical thirst is used as a symbol of spiritual longing. Both are caused by a keenly felt need. Both, if not quenched, can lead to death.

This metaphor is truly an extraordinary image in the Old Testament world. It is hard to imagine an ancient Greek philosopher thirsting for the ego-consumed god Zeus. It is unthinkable that a contemporary Canaanite could thirst for the bloodthirsty god Baal. Yet David longs for his thirst-quenching God.

God puts within us a restlessness, a neediness, a thirst for Him. But too often we respond to that need in other ways. We get anxious. We reach out for more and more money. We try to pacify ourselves with entertainment. We sooth our restlessness with the temporary thrill of buying something new.

But nothing less than God himself will ever satisfy us. God wants us to thirst for Him. That thirst should drive our prayer, our Bible reading, and yes, our church attendance. If we don't come to these means of grace with a thirst for God, we won't receive much from them.

By this thirst metaphor, the psalmist is expressing devotional commitment to the Lord. The Lord has surely been at work in his life; this divine activity is the basis for the psalmist's devotion. This devotion may be called a "purity of heart."

"Purity of heart is to will one thing, the love of God," the Danish philosopher, Søren Kierkegaard, said. It is an undiluted devotion for God that answers His free choice of us.

Prayer Is Fed by a Vision of God

Have you ever had a vision of God? I'm not talking about a physical vision that people see with their eyes or in a dream. I'm talking about a deep, personal realization of who God is, how great He is, and His immediate presence with us.

The writer of Psalm 63 had a glorious vision (v. 2). He went to the Temple and saw again God's glory, His power, and His wonderful presence with us.

The same thing happened to the writer of Psalm 73. The psalmist looks at the wicked. They never seem to have any trouble. They live as they please, ignoring God, and getting richer and richer. Life for them is a breeze.

The psalmist got envious, bitter. But then he went to the Temple, and his perspective changed. He realized that God's personal presence is life's essence and its greatest gift. Those who enjoy His presence have everything. They hold His hand throughout this life (v. 23). Afterward, they spend eternity with Him (v. 24). They need nothing else on earth or in heaven (v. 25). Those who have rejected God's presence have nothing and have doomed themselves to death (v. 27).

Our prayer life is fed and nourished by such visions of God, but these don't need to be rare events. As we turn to God in prayer, as we learn of Him in the Scriptures, as we experience Him in the Body of Believers, we get a new vision of Him. We realize He is here with us. Knowing He is present, prayer becomes a natural response to Him.

Prayer Is a Response of Praise

When I try to praise God out of obligation, because I "ought to," the words seem empty and forced. However, when I turn to Him, remembering He is with me, praise becomes the natural language of love.

I praise Him with words, spoken from my heart (63:3). I

praise Him with songs (v. 5). I want to praise Him forever (v. 4). I want to show Him I love Him by serving Him.

And I find myself not only loving God more and more, but loving those around me as well.

God is so great, so good. And praise is a natural response to standing in His presence.

David's worship is based on God's love, which is a greater good than life itself. This love is His grace, His covenant-love, which finds David and holds him unconditionally. To be loved by God in this way is "better than life" (v. 3), or to put it another way, it is to begin to live.

Steadfast love is a primary feature of God's character as a forgiving and redeeming God. In other words, the psalmist recognizes that human life depends ultimately on God's faithfulness. We often think of life in terms of biology—breathing lungs, pumping heart, etc. Other times we think of life in terms of what we do—our work, our play, our families, etc. Yet in Psalm 63, David says that God's love is better than life. God's grace and faithfulness are absolutely essential to our existence.

Prayer Is a Response of Love

We hunger for God.

We turn to Him and realize He is great, and He is with us. We respond to Him in heartfelt praise. As we live this way, we realize that walking with God is the essence of living. He is the sweetness, the joy, the pleasure of life. Our inner being becomes satisfied with Him "as with the richest of foods" (63:5).

Indeed, as I become more aware of Him, I find love for Him pouring out of my heart: "Whom have I in heaven but you? And earth has nothing I desire besides you" (73:25). "On my bed I remember you; I think of you through the watches of the night" (63:6). Day and night, every moment, in good times and in difficult times, "God is the strength of my heart and my portion forever" (73:26). "It is good to be near God" (v. 28).

Prayer is a response of love. The more we love Him, the

more precious He becomes to us and the more we want to pray.

There is an ancient tale from India about a young man who was seeking God. He went to a wise old sage for help. "How can I find God?" he asked the old man. The old man took him to a nearby river. Out they waded into the deep water. Soon the water was up just under their chins.

Suddenly the old man seized the young man by the neck and pushed him under the water. He held the young man down until the young man was flailing the water in desperation. Another few seconds and he may well have drowned.

Up out of the water the two of them came. The young man was coughing water from his lungs and still gasping for air. Reaching the bank, he asked the man indignantly, "What did that have to do with my finding God?"

The old man asked him quietly, "While you were under the water, what did you want more than anything else?"

The young man thought for a minute and then answered, "I wanted air. I wanted air more than anything else."

The old man replied, "When you want God as much as you wanted air, you will find Him."

Prayer Is a Response of Trust

I wish I could just snap my fingers and automatically trust God fully in every circumstance. However, a life of faith in all its fullness cannot be willed into existence by a solitary decision. The life of faith is a walk of faith. It must be taken one step at a time. It is a pattern of living that God teaches us day by day, trial by trial, decision by decision. It is acquired by doing.

Jesus doesn't just hand us a map, pat us on the back, and send us off on our journey. The walk of faith is a walk with Him. We're not asked to trust a God who is far away in heaven somewhere. We trust the One who is holding our hand. We trust the One who is always with us (73:23-24).

I trust my wife. I trust her enough to be myself with her. I trust her enough to share my innermost feelings with her. I trust her with my life.

That trust didn't get where it is in one day. The trust has grown from the soil of love. It's been watered by commitment and nourished by time spent together. It's meant holding on tight to her as the troubles of life try to tear us apart.

Trusting God is no different. It grows from a relationship, a love that is alive and vibrant. It develops over time, through trials and daily commitment.

God calls us to trust Him one step at a time. He asks that we turn to Him immediately when we're in need. When our daily road gets steep, He asks that we cling to Him. He wants us to realize that we find all our strength in Him. When the storms blow hard, if we trust Him, we can "sing in the shadow of [His] wings" (63:7).

When you're in need—any need—remember that God has broken down all the barriers between Him and you. You don't need to search for Him. You don't need to work up the right frame of mind. You are always in His presence. Thus, prayer can be as natural as breathing. He is constantly with us, so prayer doesn't need to stop and start. We truly can "pray continually" (1 Thessalonians 5:17).

The brilliant scientist Sir Isaac Newton said that he could take his telescope and look millions and millions of miles into space. Then he added, "But when I lay it aside, go into my room, shut the door, and get down on my knees in earnest prayer, I see more of heaven and feel closer to the Lord than if I were assisted by all the telescopes on earth."

Words to Remember: *We proclaim to you what we have seen and heard, so that you also may have fellowship with us. And our fellowship is with the Father and with his Son, Jesus Christ* (1 John 1:3).

In the morning, prayer is the key that opens to us the treasures of God's mercies and blessings; in the evening, it is the key that shuts us up under His protection and safeguard.

—Anonymous

Matthew 26

[36]Then Jesus went with his disciples to a place called Gethsemane, and he said to them, "Sit here while I go over there and pray." [37]He took Peter and the two sons of Zebedee along with him, and he began to be sorrowful and troubled. [38]Then he said to them, "My soul is overwhelmed with sorrow to the point of death. Stay here and keep watch with me."

[39]Going a little farther, he fell with his face to the ground and prayed, "My Father, if it is possible, may this cup be taken from me. Yet not as I will, but as you will."

[40]Then he returned to his disciples and found them sleeping. "Could you men not keep watch with me for one hour?" he asked Peter. [41]"Watch and pray so that you will not fall into temptation. The spirit is willing, but the body is weak."

[42]He went away a second time and prayed, "My Father, if it is not possible for this cup to be taken away unless I drink it, may your will be done."

[43]When he came back, he again found them sleeping, because their eyes were heavy. [44]So he left them and went away once more and prayed the third time, saying the same thing.

CHAPTER 2

So You Find It Difficult to Pray?

WHO FINDS IT difficult to pray? Prayer is simply conversation between us and God. Prayer simply involves honest communication. Prayer is, in part, listening for a divine response. It sounds so simple! So, who finds it difficult to pray?

I think that I hear the faintest of faint responses, almost a whisper. "Everyone." Could it be true that everyone from time to time finds it difficult to pray? Such a broad, sweeping statement surely cannot be true! Oh, it may be true of those pagan, non-Christian outsiders, but we are Christians! Could it be true that we sometimes have difficulty praying?

Let's be completely honest with ourselves and with each other. We sometimes do find it difficult to pray. This is not always the case, for there are times when prayers roll off our lips like the waves roll up on the shore. Still, there are times when it is difficult to pray, difficult to converse with God, difficult to be open and vulnerable before the Almighty, difficult to listen.

Whether the difficulty springs from life-circumstances, feelings of inadequacy, feelings of guilt, bashfulness, or mental blocks, this chapter provides ways we can overcome some of these barriers to effective prayer.

Our examination begins with a look at Jesus as He was at prayer in the Garden of Gethsemane. More specifically, we focus on the disciples in that scene. In the midst of one of the most difficult times for Jesus, they failed to pray with Him. We wonder why. The proper thing, the "spiritual" thing, would have been for them to recognize Jesus' anguish and share His load by praying fervently with Him. They missed a great opportunity to be "prayer warriors" by falling asleep that night. Before we're too hard on the disciples, however, we must recognize how they reflect our own behavior all too often. We don't always pray when we should.

However, we can turn to James for practical help in this matter. James shows us some prayers are not answered because they are never prayed. He reveals how improper motives make our prayers ineffective. And he gives us wise advice—spend more time in God's presence in order to confound the powers of the devil.

Sweet Hour of Prayer?

"Sweet Hour of Prayer" is one of those songs I associate with my youth. We had a recording of it on an old Pat Boone album. (Now that really dates me!) His mellow tones reflected the tranquil scene described in the words of the song. It portrayed peaceful, almost effortless communion with God. In those moments of prayer, we find relief and joy. It is a time of shared communion, not only with God but also with others who join in bearing our burden of prayer. The prospect of this prayer retreat is met with anxious gladness and full of confident expectation of blessing. What a beautiful picture. Unfortunately, my own experience doesn't always have such blissful character.

Sometimes I find it difficult to pray. I have had times in prayer like the experience portrayed in the song. I enjoy and treasure them. Nevertheless, all of my prayer experience isn't like that. Sometimes prayer is hard work. Sometimes it isn't a mountaintop experience. There are even times (dare I admit it?) when I don't feel much like praying at all. There are times I don't know how to pray, and even if I do pray it doesn't seem like God is listening. I confess that these experiences wouldn't make a very inspiring hymn, but they are my experiences. They may be your experiences too. We need to figure out what do with them and how to understand them.

I'm glad that Scripture includes portrayals of prayer that can help us. Two of those passages are the subjects of this chapter. Both deal with some of the difficult issues in prayer.

The first lesson we draw from these scriptures is that it is OK to face difficulty in prayer. What a relief! If the apostles struggled in prayer, then perhaps I can be less hard on myself if I do too. So, relieved of the burden of some false guilt, let's be overcomers in our prayer journey.

Hindrances to Prayer

Matthew's account of Jesus at Gethsemane and James's teaching in chapter 4 highlight several hindrances to prayer. Physical fatigue was a simple but important factor in the disciple's failure to persist in prayer with Jesus in the Garden. When we are weary, it is harder to pray. The detailed account of Jesus' struggle in prayer portrays a very different scene than the peaceful "Sweet Hour of Prayer." We observe a labor in prayer that was even physical in its effort. Sometimes prayer is real work.

Jesus prayed alone. There was no faithful circle of like-minded prayer partners. His closest companions were asleep. In one of the most heartrending accounts in Scripture, Jesus was abandoned as He faced the lonely call to the Cross.

Both James and Jesus faced the question of unanswered prayer or at least coming to terms with a different answer than we would choose. Jesus struggled to accept the answer His Father was giving. James specifically addressed the problem of wrong motives in prayer. They hinder both the prayer and the response. James recognized Satan's interference as the backdrop of many struggles in prayer. Satan can't be expected to respect our "Do Not Disturb" sign as we go to prayer.

This is not offered as a comprehensive list. There are surely more hindrances to prayer that we could identify from our experiences and observations. They do serve, however, to underscore the challenge of prayer and the difficulties to over-come. Praying with increased effectiveness will require us to address these issues. We recognize that they are there; now, how do we overcome them?

Developing an Overcoming Prayer Life

Part of the message that should become clear is that an ef-fective prayer life doesn't just happen. It is more than just an effortless experience of God's blessing. There are real obstacles to overcome. Prayer is a challenging spiritual exercise involving commitment, discipline, and spiritual focus. As we work to make that a reality, we want to consider some practical issues, the question of perspective, and the "heart" of the matter.

Practical Issues

Thinking about practical strategies for prayer may not seem very spiritual, but it is, nonetheless, of critical impor-tance. The fatigue of the disciples in the garden is a good ex-ample of how the practical matters of the flesh interfere with the desires of the spirit. It is not really spiritual to ignore prac-tical concerns; it is shortsighted and probably foolish. We should work to build patterns of behavior into our lifestyle that help us pray, rather than posing obstacles to overcome. One obvious lesson is to try to come to prayer rested and physically refreshed. If we plan our prayer time at the end of an exhausting day, we are headed for difficulties. If we stay up late watching television and then try to get up early for prayer time, we are programmed for failure. No matter how intensely we try to focus our spiritual energy, the flesh will be weak.

If the plan is to pray in the morning, we should go to bed early. If we plan to pray in the evening, we should save some time and energy when still alert and fresh. We will not always be able to come to prayer rested and fresh, but we should do our best to try.

We must try to make lifestyle patterns work for and not against us. A morning person should plan his or her prayer time in the morning. A night person should plan to pray at night. Those who are easily disturbed should find a quiet place. If the best personal time is while commuting, plan to pray while driving (eyes open, please!). There is no benefit in making prayer as difficult as possible.

Is prayer time losing its freshness? Creativity in prayer is allowed. Sing a hymn. Pray a psalm. We can pray on our knees, on our faces, standing up, or sitting down. One of my favorite ways to spend time with God is early in the morning, sitting in a chair that looks out a window, drinking my morning coffee. Sometimes that is the best part of my day. Why wouldn't I want to share that time with God?

If we find ourselves distracted by remembering things we need to do, keep a notepad close by. Take a moment to write a brief reminder and go back to prayer time.

The Question of Perspective

Developing a prayer life that overcomes requires approaching prayer with the right perspective. It starts with an understanding that prayer involves intentional effort and discipline. An effective prayer life doesn't just happen by accident.

If we are passive in our approach to prayer, we will be inconsistent and superficial. Discipline is not a popular concept in our society, but it is a necessary component of successful prayer. It means that we pray "on purpose." We are intentional in our practice of prayer. It also means that we will learn to pray and grow more effective in prayer over time. It is a process that will continue for as long as we live.

The right perspective for prayer also involves a focus on God and not on others. Jesus had to set aside the failure of His disciples and focus His prayer on the Father. So do we.

Prayer that is preoccupied with what we think others should be doing or not doing will be ineffective. We need to focus our attention on God and let that focus shape our perspective in prayer. He will help us sort out everything else in the right way.

The Heart of the Matter

Overcoming prayer begins with the heart. Our prayers will be more effective when we start with the right attitude. Our ability to deal with apparently unanswered prayer or different answers than we anticipated will depend on the same right attitude. We have to answer a fundamental question concerning our approach to prayer. Is prayer about bringing our world into line with God's plan or getting God to help us bring our world in line with our plan?

If a person's prayers are simply for the things that will gratify his or her desires, these prayers are essentially selfish. Therefore, it is not possible for God to answer them. The true end of prayer is to say to God, "Your will be done." The prayer of the person who is pleasure-dominated is, "My desires be satisfied." It is a fact of life that we can't pray appropriately until we take ourselves from the center of our lives and put God there.

If prayer is about getting God to help us do what we want, then our prayer life is going to struggle. When God doesn't do what we think should be done, we will be impatient and disappointed. God is not like a magic genie, granting our wishes when we rub the lamp the right way. Our God is far greater than that. His will is always for our best and for the best of those we love.

James gave us some sound and effective counsel when he wrote "Come near to God and he will come near to you" (4:8). When we draw near to God in prayer, then we begin to discover an overcoming prayer life. That means our approach to prayer involves bringing a listening ear, a teachable spirit, and a responsive heart. When our attitude is right, we are on track for a prayer life that can handle the difficulties along the way.

Sweet Hour of Prayer!

Standing at the South Pole is like being in the eye of a hurricane—it's deceivingly calm. The quietness seems inconsistent with the fact that mighty winds originate there. How is this possible? As warm air from the equator flows in over the polar region, it descends, becomes cold and dense, and sinks to the frigid surface. Since the ice-covered plateau tapers off toward the oceans, and no mountains or other obstacles stand in the way, gravity pulls the heavy, cold air down the smooth slopes. The wind picks up tremendous speed as it moves northward toward the equator. Gradually, it is heated by the sun and begins to rise, creating a circular pattern to drive the earth's weather machine.

For Christians, quiet times of prayer and worship also give rise to great power. Our urge is almost compulsive: do, work, worry, and struggle. Yet, at the heart of accomplishing things for God must be that regular experience of calm followed by an unobstructed flow of energy.

Prayer is a challenging spiritual exercise. It requires our best and wisest effort, commitment, and discipline. It both requires and produces a right spiritual attitude and focus. It will not always result in a changed situation, but it will surely change us.

Difficulties in prayer? Sure. But we don't let a few obstacles and a little hard work keep us from the rich rewards of prayer. Whether we are in peaceful times of blessing or tormented by a storm, the time we invest with God is always a sweet hour of prayer.

Words to Remember: *Watch and pray so that you will not fall into temptation. The spirit is willing, but the body is weak* (Matthew 26:41).

I used to pray that God would do this or that.
Now I pray that God will make His will known to
me. —Mme. Chiang Kai-shek

Matthew 6

[5]"And when you pray, do not be like the hypocrites, for they love to pray standing in the synagogues and on the street corners to be seen by men. I tell you the truth, they have received their reward in full. [6]But when you pray, go into your room, close the door and pray to your Father, who is unseen. Then your Father, who sees what is done in secret, will reward you. [7]And when you pray, do not keep on babbling like pagans, for they think they will be heard because of their many words. [8]Do not be like them, for your Father knows what you need before you ask him.

[9]"This, then, is how you should pray:

'Our Father in heaven,
hallowed be your name,
[10]your kingdom come,
your will be done
on earth as it is in heaven.'"

Psalm 145

[1]I will exalt you, my God the King;
I will praise your name for ever and ever.
[2]Every day I will praise you
and extol your name for ever and ever.

[3]Great is the LORD and most worthy of praise;
his greatness no one can fathom.
[4]One generation will commend your works to another;
they will tell of your mighty acts.
[5]They will speak of the glorious splendor of your majesty,
and I will meditate on your wonderful works.
[6]They will tell of the power of your awesome works,
and I will proclaim your great deeds.
[7]They will celebrate your abundant goodness
and joyfully sing of your righteousness. . . .

[21]My mouth will speak in praise of the LORD.
Let every creature praise his holy name
for ever and ever.

CHAPTER 3

Hallowed Be Your Name

MANY CHRISTIAN PEOPLE struggle to find a proper balance in their relationship to God, especially as it relates to their prayer life. On the one hand, God's love and compassion have been emphasized in our churches. Preaching and teaching have spotlighted how close we can be to God because of His loving and compassionate nature. We have learned that God is kind, God is merciful, and that He wants to be our Friend.

Such teaching has been a helpful correction to the other side of the issue—namely, that God is remote and not very concerned about the daily needs of human beings. However, such an emphasis on God's friendliness may have caused us to forget or downplay His equally important characteristics of holiness and majesty. The God who came to earth in the form of a baby is the same God who, with a word, created the universe and all that is in it.

Perhaps we can restore a needed balance to our view of God as we listen to both Jesus and the psalmist David place emphasis on the majesty of God. The message is clear: God *is* approachable, but He is still an awesome God whose name we hallow.

Within the Sermon on the Mount, Jesus teaches us *how* to pray as well as *what* to pray. He prefaced His model prayer with specific instructions to His disciples about how to pray.

He told them to pray to the Father in secret, unlike others who make repetitive and public vain prayers. Then He taught them to begin prayer by showing proper respect to God the Father.

In this chapter, we will examine Jesus' instructions that help us pray in a right manner rather than like those who only *think* their prayers are being heard. We will note Jesus' emphasis on the holiness, majesty, and sacredness of the One to whom we pray. The psalmist will also help reawaken our appreciation by showing us a detailed example of meditation on God's majesty.

We will focus our attention on the first half of the Lord's model prayer. In the next chapter we will concentrate on the second half. We need to study the example Jesus gave us in two discussions because we cannot truly ask for the right things until we fully understand as much as possible about the Person to whom we are praying.

Beginning to Pray

The introduction to the Lord's Prayer continues to amaze us. We know that the Jews had developed a detailed structure for their prayer lives. The historical records provide prescribed prayers for nearly every occasion. The New Testament records indicate that they continued to carry out these prescriptions with great care.

In Luke's record, the disciples of our Lord come to Him with the surprising request that He teach them to pray in the way in which John the Baptist had taught his disciples to pray. We can assume that they wanted to be able to pray in a way that would reflect the primary focus and direction of their Master. Our Lord responded to their request with a surprisingly simple and powerful prayer.

Matthew records the Lord's Prayer in the middle of the Sermon on the Mount. All of this is part of the foundational pattern for persons who "seek first [God's] kingdom and his righteousness" (6:33), the highest priority for Christians. They are "Beatitude people," who live out the intent of the Law instead of merely trying to escape through loopholes in the Law. They model themselves after the perfect "heavenly Father" (5:48). They do not pray out loud just to gain the approval of those standing near by (6:1-4). They pray to the Father in secret. They are fruitful doers of the Word.

In such a context, Jesus invites His disciples to spend extended time with the Heavenly Father in order to truly become Kingdom people.

The Beauty of Simplicity

The prayer is amazingly simple and short—especially in comparison to the complicated prayers of the Jews. There are only about 70 words (whether we are counting in Greek or English) in the model prayer when we include the doxology. Jesus was serious when He scolded them not to "keep on babbling like pagans" (6:7), who assume that many words and rich language will capture God's attention. Jesus was serious when He chastised the hypocrites who pray in full view of others in order to gain attention.

The Lord's Prayer begins with a simple and direct address to God, "Our Father in heaven." "Father" stands first in the Greek text to emphasize the spiritual intimacy existing between Jesus and the Father. The Greek text reflects the underlying Aramaic in which "Father" is a term of familiarity and intimacy, "Abba" or "Papa." This opening word is an invitation to address God directly.

The opening word is immediately followed by the plural "our." We come to the Father in fellowship with our elder brother, Jesus, who taught us to pray. We come to the Father in community with all who make the Kingdom their highest priority. It is very significant that in the Lord's Prayer the words "I," "me," "my," and "mine" never occur; Jesus came to take these words out of life and to put in their place "we," "us," and "ours." God is not any person's exclusive possession.

The words "in heaven" protect us from taking advantage of this invitation to intimacy. God is not a cosmic bellhop whom we can manipulate. He is the Creator God of the universe who seeks to enter into relationship with us.

There is a freedom and simplicity in the Lord's Prayer when our attention is focused upon God. The remainder of the first half of the Lord's Prayer is also focused upon God himself. Persons who follow Christ as Master do not focus first upon themselves. They deliberately gaze upon God and meditate on His perfect will. Then all else falls into proper place.

There are interesting evidences of our failure to follow the model that our Lord has given us. Many persons pray extended prayers for purposes of gaining attention. One historian referred to a particular prayer as "one of the greatest prayers ever offered to a Boston audience." Others pray their prayers in the third person, until it is obvious they are not speaking *to* God but only speaking *about* God.

The simplicity and freedom of the Lord's Prayer invites us all into a rich relationship with God in prayer. Our Lord not only taught us how to pray but modeled such a life as well. His witness in the Gospel of John affirms that relationship at every point. "The words I say to you are not just my own. Rather, it is the Father, living in me, who is doing his work" (14:10). His focus was on God—and God alone—in spiritual intimacy.

Hallowed Be Your Name

In the first petition of the Lord's Prayer, our Lord invites us to pray that God's name may be hallowed and honored above all else. Jesus was following the model that we also see in the Psalms.

Psalm 145 emphasizes such a focus upon God. The psalmist recognizes God as the source of all goodness and grace and compassion and glory. Awe and praise will characterize anyone who recognizes and exalts God as the psalmist prescribes. Not only will people open their mouths to speak "in praise of the LORD" (v. 21), but they will invite others to participate in that praise as well.

Prayer that hastens to the request section signals a fundamental shift in relationship with God. God is no longer the primary focus; personal needs have taken primacy. When personal needs are more important than celebrating God's gracious compassion and goodness, a form of selfishness becomes visible. Prayer changes from nurturing a relationship with God to a demand for divine condescension for our needs. Genuine prayer is a purposeful focus upon God without drawing attention to ourselves.

To pray "hallowed be your name" colors all of our praying and our living. It has been said that the Lord's Prayer is like a bomb ticking in church, waiting to explode and demolish our temples to false gods. It is a revolutionary petition to invite God to make His name holy and honored in the world.

I often wonder what we expect to happen when we pray this prayer. Do we expect the world to shift on its axis? Do we expect powerful lightning and thunder to echo across the sky? Do we expect God is going to make a fundamental shift in our own way of thinking and living?

Or do we simply pray with minimal expectations? Are we like the person who prayed for a mountain to be removed but the next morning went to the window and observed, "Just as I expected—nothing happened"?

To pray is to set our sights on God—and God alone—in anticipation that He will break through in unexpected and powerful ways. To pray is to spend time in God's presence, allowing Him to change us in the process.

Are you as surprised as I am that this first petition of the Lord's Prayer invites God to make a positive breakthrough in our world? The first focus of praying is to exalt God and invite Him to change our world—and us.

When Martin Luther was commenting on this petition, he used the analogy of a stone lying in the sun. It is unnecessary to command such a stone to be warm. Warmth is a natural by-product of resting in the sun day after day. It is easy to extend this analogy to the way in which we pray. It is unnecessary to command the person who spends extended time in God's presence, using the model of the Lord's Prayer, to be holy. Holiness of life is the normal by-product of living in His presence and nurturing a relationship with Him through prayer.

The Importance of a Name

In the Old Testament culture, the name was the key to the essence of the person. When God revealed His name to Moses, "I AM WHO I AM" (Exodus 3:14), the Hebrews began to understand the essential nature of the God who was guiding them. They began to worship Him in light of who He was and the mighty acts by which He displayed His mercy and compassion to them.

To pray essentially "let your name be made holy" is to worship God for who He is and to anticipate the mighty deeds by which He will make himself known in our contemporary world. To pray that prayer in the morning is to anticipate that God will make himself known before the sun sets.

When we grasp the full meaning of *name* as signifying the personality of the bearer, we get a glimpse of the seriousness of taking the Lord's name in vain. To profane His name is to live in such a way that others are unable to know God as He really is.

Submission and Praise

This early segment of the Lord's Prayer is deepened and extended when we turn to the next two petitions: "Your kingdom come, your will be done on earth as it is in heaven" (6:9). The person who has regularly prayed that God would hallow His name—make His name highly visible and clearly distinctive—is ready for God's kingdom and God's will to be done on earth as it is in heaven.

Prayer is a ready submission to the total design of God—for the world and for ourselves. When we have become increasingly aware of His holy presence through prayer, the options of submission and repentance are not difficult and burdensome. Instead these options are welcomed. We can hardly wait for God to make His kingdom clearly visible and powerfully present. We join with God's priorities in wanting His perfect will to be done.

Jesus used the living illustration of the child in Matthew

18:3-4 to highlight the submission, trust, and obedience that are characteristic of Kingdom people. The childlike faith of the person who lives out the Beatitudes expects personal kingdoms to be set aside in order that God may further His. The implicit trust of the person who has prayed for God to hallow His name anticipates that God's saving will take precedence over personal plans and designs.

Conclusion

Our Lord taught us to pray with freedom and intimacy to a God who makes a difference in our world. Praise and submission are the primary language of the Kingdom.

The Lord's Prayer is an invitation for us to spend enough time with the Father until our lives reflect His kingdom and will. To nurture a relationship with God according to the pattern that Jesus provides for us will change our lives and the way we pray. Even the tone of voice and the pattern of dialogue with the Father will change.

I have a friend who works in an office that has dividers instead of walls between the desks. He observed that he could identify the person on the other end of the telephone conversation by the tone of voice and pattern of conversation used by a colleague. Talking to a client, talking to a friend, or conversation with a spouse all had different tones and patterns.

The question for us today is: How does our pattern of conversation in prayer reflect the quality of our relationship with God?

Words to Remember: *One day Jesus was praying in a certain place. When he finished, one of his disciples said to him, "Lord, teach us to pray, just as John taught his disciples"* (Luke 11:1).

To pray . . . is to desire, but it is to desire what God would have us desire. He who desires not from the bottom of his heart offers a deceitful prayer.

—Fénelon

Matthew 6

¹¹Give us today our daily bread.
¹²Forgive us our debts,
    as we also have forgiven our debtors.
¹³And lead us not into temptation,
but deliver us from the evil one.

¹⁴For if you forgive men when they sin against you, your heavenly Father will also forgive you. ¹⁵But if you do not forgive men their sins, your Father will not forgive your sins. . . .

²⁵"Therefore I tell you, do not worry about your life, what you will eat or drink; or about your body, what you will wear. Is not life more important than food, and the body more important than clothes? ²⁶Look at the birds of the air; they do not sow or reap or store away in barns, and yet your heavenly Father feeds them. Are you not much more valuable than they? ²⁷Who of you by worrying can add a single hour to his life?

²⁸"And why do you worry about clothes? See how the lilies of the field grow. They do not labor or spin. ²⁹Yet I tell you that not even Solomon in all his splendor was dressed like one of these. ³⁰If that is how God clothes the grass of the field, which is here today and tomorrow is thrown into the fire, will he not much more clothe you, O you of little faith? ³¹So do not worry, saying, 'What shall we eat?' or 'What shall we drink?' or 'What shall we wear?' ³²For the pagans run after all these things, and your heavenly Father knows that you need them. ³³But seek first his kingdom and his righteousness, and all these things will be given to you as well. ³⁴Therefore do not worry about tomorrow, for tomorrow will worry about itself. Each day has enough trouble of its own."

CHAPTER 4

Give Us Our Daily Bread

WHY DO INDIVIDUALS living in the wealthiest regions of the world need to discuss "needs"? Because the ancient confession, "O Lord, we are a needy people!" is true of *all* people. Social standing does not matter; economic resources do not matter; intellectual prowess does not matter. All people are needy.

Granted, our economic and political circumstances are different from the circumstances of Jesus' audience. However, there are commonalties that transcend historical and geographical particulars. We are all in need of the "bread of heaven" (Psalm 105:40). We are all in need of forgiveness. We all must be reminded that there are those around us who are also needy. We all should recognize that we cannot control the events and circumstances of our lives. We are a needy people!

The Lord's Prayer is an expression of faith, not only in what it says but in what it assumes. These verses are not a command to pray or a scolding for not praying; they assume that people do pray. The assumption is that human beings are not self-sufficient. It is not a sign of weakness to pray but a sign of genuine humanity. Prayer is not merely for emergencies but is thankful praise that acknowledges our dependence on God.

In the previous chapter, we concentrated on the primary focus of our prayer—God the Father. We regained a sense of awe as we considered the majesty of God. We discovered how vital it is to orient our prayers within the context of God's will and His kingdom. We found it an important exercise to pause and ponder the opening address of the model prayer that Jesus gave His disciples.

In this chapter, we move even deeper as we explore our relationship with God in prayer through confession of need and failure. Not only does God want to give us all the physical things we need—food, clothing, and shelter—but He also wants to supply our deepest spiritual needs.

We move from meditating on God's greatness to realizing two important aspects of our relationship with Him: We have needs that only God can fulfill. And God, in His gracious and abundant love for us, wants to meet our needs. Those truths become evident to us in the second half of the Lord's Prayer.

The person whose primary focus is upon God and the things of the Kingdom will ask for personal needs and desires in the appropriate fashion and sequence. The same basic trust, which anticipates the coming of the Kingdom, makes it easier to trust God for our personal needs.

Prayer as an Expression of Trust

My mother was a worrywart. She not only worried about all of the normal things, she borrowed things to worry about. One day I tried to chide her on the basis of this section from the Sermon on the Mount. I noted that worry never solved any problems. I suggested that worry was an obvious lack of trust. I can still see the hurt look on her face as I talked.

Matthew 6:24, "You cannot serve both God and Money," helps set the context for the verses that follow on worry about things. The word translated "money" in this verse is the Greek word "mammon," which has a variety of meanings, including that of "property." In this case, mammon would include the kinds of things we are told not to worry about in verses 25-34.

In this portion of the Sermon on the Mount, Jesus calls for complete trust in the Heavenly Father. Worry is to be replaced by resting in the grace of God's total provision for us.

The Lord uses a number of analogies to describe the kind of trust the Christian normally exhibits. In verse 26, He uses the example of the birds of the air. They live an apparently carefree life. They do not work at sowing, reaping, and storing. They flit about in complete confidence that God will care for them.

In verse 28, He uses the example of the lilies of the field. They do not spend time worrying about anything but are more beautiful than Solomon in all his splendor. The relatively short term of their beauty does not create any concern (v. 30).

When Jesus tells us not to worry, He is not advocating a reckless, thoughtless attitude toward life; He is bidding us to leave behind a way of life that is burdened with fear and care, one which takes all the joy out of living.

The invitation to trust God completely is emphasized by the series of rhetorical questions throughout verses 25-34. In verse 25 the question forces the hearer to admit that life is more important than food and the body is far more important that the clothing which it carries. In verse 26, the hearer has to admit that human beings are far more valuable than the birds that trust God so implicitly. In verse 27, everyone has to acknowledge that worrying will not add length to life; in fact, worry may make it shorter.

Verse 28 returns to the issue of clothes and asks why Christians spend so much time worrying about what they will wear. In verse 30, Jesus invites His hearers to believe that God will exhibit greater care for eternal beings than He will for the temporary grass and flowers.

The final assurance in this invitation to trust is that the Heavenly Father, who cares for grass and birds and flowers, knows precisely what we need. Pagans who are unaware that God has such detailed knowledge of our needs are justified in worrying. Christians who know their God need to trust Him implicitly.

Prayer is, then, not so much an issue of telling God what we need, as it is an exercise in trusting God's gracious provisions for the Kingdom and His righteousness, as well as for everyday needs. The patterns and sequences of our prayers change drastically when we are no longer frantically trying to gain God's attention. Prayer becomes a way to nurture our relationship with God. Prayer becomes a way to soak in grace until our lives reflect the Father who is in heaven. Prayer becomes a conversation with a dear Friend who is waiting to provide.

When we look at the structure of our prayers, it quickly becomes apparent that we seldom pray with complete trust. We plead and struggle as we pray. We are not completely confident that God knows and will provide.

Each of us has known mature Christians who have lived the way the Sermon on the Mount prescribes. There is an aura of peace about them. They walk confidently in God's gracious provisions. They never panic, for they know God is with them.

Such an understanding of the way God works releases us from the burden of carrying the whole universe on our shoulders. It frees us to live and to pray the way our Lord taught us to pray.

Trusting for Daily Bread

The pattern our Lord provided asks us first to pray that His name would be hallowed, set apart, and made holy in every aspect of life. Then we are instructed to offer ourselves in submission that His kingdom might come. The third petition focuses upon the total saving will of God in our world. Trust and submission—and even repentance—were clearly implied in opening our prayers as Jesus taught us.

Only after these three grand petitions have been prayed are we instructed to pray for daily bread. The sequence is striking. Surely the person who is able to trust God to hallow His name, send His kingdom, and do His perfect will can trust God for daily bread.

The Greek word used here for "daily" is a rare form. The extraordinary fact about this word is that, until a short time ago, there was no other known occurrence of this word in the whole of Greek literature. It was therefore not possible to be sure what it meant. However, a papyrus fragment turned up with this word on it. The fragment was actually a woman's shopping list with this rare word next to an item on it. It was a note to remind her to buy a certain food item for the coming day. So now we know that this petition means, "Give me the things I need to eat *for this coming day.* Help me to get the things on my shopping list when I go out this morning."

Many commentators have insisted that "bread" should be taken metaphorically and spiritually. They believe the Lord must be talking about something other than physical bread after such grand and far-reaching petitions.

Yet when we reflect on the economy of the first century, it is plain that He was speaking of physical bread. When we look at the rest of the chapter, it is clear that trusting God for daily provisions is the primary point of this petition.

In an affluent world, it is often difficult to trust God for such basic necessities when we are usually able to provide them by our own budgeted energy and means. Again, the rest of this chapter points out distinctly that we must recognize that everything comes from God—and God alone. Then even our table prayers become expressions of our implicit trust in God.

It is sad that fast foods have robbed modern families of the learning and shaping experience of giving God thanks for daily bread. We have become much better at complaining about food than blessing it. The words of Isaiah 1:3 to Israel still ring true: "The ox knows his master, the donkey his owner's manger, but Israel does not know, my people do not understand." We are an ungrateful people who worry about food and drink and clothes, because we do not regularly acknowledge the Source of all supply.

Trusting for Forgiveness

The pattern of the Lord's Prayer moves from understanding the grace of daily bread to the grace of reconciling relationships—forgiveness. It requires as much trust in God's grace to receive forgiveness as it does to trust totally for daily bread. In the original Greek, bread and forgiveness are joined by the first appearance of the word "and" in the prayer. ("And" appears at the beginning of verse 12 of KJV but not NIV.)

Forgiveness was an important theme in the life and teaching of our Lord. The extension of forgiveness to those who murdered Him on the Cross makes the centrality of forgiveness in the model prayer even more powerful.

Jesus cut to the heart of the issue when He tied forgiveness and daily bread together in this profound prayer. When we do not have physical bread to eat, we die. When we do not have the grace of forgiveness functioning in our lives, we die emotionally and spiritually.

Again, the Lord's Prayer brings us to the place where we learn to trust God and His grace without question. We have to be totally honest. Praying is an openness before God that permits us to bring every type of petition to Him. There is no hurt too deep for us to utter in prayer. There is no pain that cannot be touched and healed by our Father.

When we learn to pray for forgiveness with the same naturalness with which we pray for daily bread, life will certainly change. When we trust God to provide reconciling love in the same breath that we give thanks for our food, prayer will indeed become a way of life.

Trusting for Deliverance

The final petition of the Lord's Prayer is a double-barreled one. "And lead us not into temptation, but deliver us from the evil one" (v. 13).

Again, the presence of the word "and" before this petition is emphatic. Just as daily bread and forgiveness are tied together by the word "and," so this final petition is tied very closely to both bread and forgiveness. The whole sequence of the Lord's Prayer is underlined. Prayers that begin with a focus upon God—His holy name, His kingdom, and His total will—move naturally to daily bread and forgiveness. Deliverance from testing and temptation flow naturally from the earlier segment of the prayer.

Our Lord himself not only teaches us how to pray but also offers us a wonderful model in His life. The temptation, recorded in both Matthew 4 and Luke 4, reveals a Master who understood how to trust the Father in major testing at the beginning of His public ministry. The Garden of Gethsemane describes a person who was able to trust God implicitly as He faced the Cross. He prayed, "Father, if you are willing, take this cup from me; yet not my will, but yours be done" (Luke 22:42).

The Father, who so graciously responds to our total trust in Him, will certainly deliver us from the temptations to which we are prone. When we come to the place that we are able to trust God for the grand things of the Kingdom as well as the daily necessities of our lives, we then learn to trust Him for areas of weakness and temptation and compromise. What a way to live and to pray!

Words to Remember: *Cast your cares on the* LORD *and he will sustain you; he will never let the righteous fall* (Psalm 55:22).

Our prayer and God's mercy are like two buckets in a well; while the one ascends the other descends.
—Mark Hopkins

Psalm 51

[1]Have mercy on me, O God,
   according to your unfailing love;
according to your great compassion
   blot out my transgressions.
[2]Wash away all my iniquity
   and cleanse me from my sin.

[3]For I know my transgressions,
   and my sin is always before me.
[4]Against you, you only, have I sinned
   and done what is evil in your sight,
so that you are proved right when you speak
   and justified when you judge.
[5]Surely I was sinful at birth,
   sinful from the time my mother conceived me.
[6]Surely you desire truth in the inner parts;
   you teach me wisdom
   in the inmost place.

[7]Cleanse me with hyssop, and I will be clean;
   wash me, and I will be whiter than snow.
[8]Let me hear joy and gladness;
   let the bones you have crushed rejoice.
[9]Hide your face from my sins
   and blot out all my iniquity.

[10]Create in me a pure heart, O God,
   and renew a steadfast spirit within me.
[11]Do not cast me from your presence
   or take your Holy Spirit from me.
[12]Restore to me the joy of your salvation
   and grant me a willing spirit, to sustain me.

[13]Then I will teach transgressors your ways,
   and sinners will turn back to you.
[14]Save me from bloodguilt, O God,
   the God who saves me,
   and my tongue will sing of your righteousness.
[15]O Lord, open my lips,
   and my mouth will declare your praise.

[16]You do not delight in sacrifice, or I would bring it;
   you do not take pleasure in burnt offerings.
[17]The sacrifices of God are a broken spirit;
   a broken and contrite heart,
   O God, you will not despise.

CHAPTER 5

Have Mercy on Me, O God

DO WE BELIEVE this statement: "Confession is an appropriate activity for believers"? In our tradition, it is more likely that we think confession is something an unbeliever does in order to be converted to Christ. Why should persons who are already Christians examine the concept of confession?

The answer can be summed up in one word—failure. Because Christians are human, we fall short. We *want* to speak, think, and act in perfectly Christlike ways. However, things go wrong. We sometimes say things without realizing how hurtful our words are to others. Sometimes we misjudge someone's motives. Sometimes we make a mistake despite our best intention to do right. And, sometimes we as Christians even deliberately choose to disobey God and fall into willful sin.

The act of confessing to God opens us to the scrutiny of the Holy Spirit. His examination of our hearts will give a true verdict. In confession, we bring our failures and disappointments to God and ask, "Have I sinned?" If the Holy Spirit tells us yes, we can find forgiveness and peace. If He tells us no, so much the better; we can move on from our failures. No one was ever saddened by a "clean bill of health."

Because failure is always a possibility in this fallen world, confession gives us the correct (that is, humble) attitude toward God. We place ourselves in a position to receive grace from God rather than let life's problems block our relationship with Him.

Is the fact that God is great and gives to us like a father as far as our relationship with God goes? No. The relationship we cultivate through prayer goes beyond that. God is interested in a continuing relationship. He wants to hear about our disappointments and needs, but He wants to hear about our failures as well. He wants to sustain us when we fail—even if we sin.

In this chapter we examine David's confession of sin in Psalm 51. In it, he models a proper attitude for Christians to have toward God. Confession reveals our understanding of God. To confess that we have failed—or even sinned—shows that we believe God is approachable, compassionate, and forgiving. The practice of confessing to God keeps us honest about our lives. We are less likely to live with illusions and denial in our lives if we regularly allow God to examine our hearts. Confession puts us in a proper place to receive whatever our spirits need—forgiveness, restoration, or affirmation.

Though David had definite sin to confess—his adultery with Bathsheba and his murder of Uriah (see 2 Samuel 11—12)—his model is helpful for us in confessing either outright sin or simple failure. Because we are human, we will sometimes fall short of how we try to live. Still, we can bring our broken pieces to God and experience forgiveness and peace.

Jesus gave His followers a prayer that beautifully models an open, dependent relationship with God our Father. This model prayer includes the words, "Forgive us."

We are too often weak and inconsistent. We sometimes think and act more selfishly than we admit or even realize. God, in contrast, is always loving, pure, and holy. If we are to maintain an open, honest relationship with a God of such qualities, confession must be part of that relationship.

As we get closer to God, we become more conscious of our weaknesses. In the presence of a holy, loving God, we realize how very much we need Him. He expects us to handle this need as all our needs—by bringing it to Him.

We don't have to wait. We don't have to decide if what

we've done is a "sin" or just a human shortcoming. Our Father wants us to bring our needs and our weaknesses to Him in simple, childlike faith.

Praying for Forgiveness

Do you know what guilt feels like? Of course, you do. We all do. We know the heaviness. We know the shadow on our hearts. We sense the stain that we just can't wash away. When we feel this guilt, we can deal with it in various ways.

Sometimes we try to ignore the guilt, hoping it will go away. "I just won't dwell on it. I'll get busy again, and eventually I'll forget it ever happened."

Sometimes we try to minimize what we've done. "It really isn't that bad. Most people do a lot worse than me."

Sometimes we try to excuse it. "It's just the way my parents raised me. Society is trying to force its standards on me. If I ignore the rules, I'll soon get past this feeling."

Sometimes we try to make up for what we've done. "I'll be especially kind to people. I'll do good deeds. That will make up for my wrong. Maybe my good deeds will outweigh the bad."

Or maybe we feel our sin is so bad that we can't let ourselves off the hook easily. So we clutch our sin, savor the shame, and try to prove how sorry we are.

Psalm 51 is one of the best models of repentance in all of Scripture. The writer, David, didn't handle his guilt in any of the above ways.

There's no denial in his first words. "Have mercy on me, O God" (v. 1).

There's no ignoring or hiding. "I know my transgressions, and my sin is always before me" (v. 3).

There's no excusing, rationalizing, or blaming others. "Against you, you only, have I sinned and done what is evil in your sight, so that you are proved right when you speak and justified when you judge" (v. 4).

There's no attempt to minimize his guilt. "I am sinful to the core, Lord. I've been a sinner my entire life" (v. 5, author's paraphrase).

David is like a criminal throwing himself completely on the mercy of the court. His only appeal is to God's "unfailing love" and "great compassion" (v. 1). In the depths of his need, he trusts God enough to cling to His grace. Though completely unworthy, he obeys God by claiming His promises.

He asks God to "blot out" his sin (vv. 1, 9). He prays that He would "wash away" all his iniquity, as one would wash dirty clothes (v. 2). The second verb used in this petition for forgiveness ("cleanse") seems to be derived from the domestic practice of washing clothes and does not refer, primarily, to bathing. The usage for washing clothes accords with the basic meaning of the Hebrew verb, which is "to tread" or "to pummel," since clothes were washed by beating or treading them in water.

David asks all this in complete confidence. "Cleanse me with hyssop, and I will be clean; wash me, and I will be whiter than snow" (v. 7).

This is what our Father wants of us when we fail. Yes, we do feel unworthy. Yes, we know we don't deserve forgiveness. Still, He wants us to claim His promise in simple trust. The New Testament version of this concept is, "If we confess our sins, he is faithful and just and will forgive us our sins and purify us from all unrighteousness" (1 John 1:9).

We please God by coming in obedience. We please Him by trusting Him enough to confess openly from our heart. In His love, He delights to forgive us and embrace us again. "I have swept away your offenses like a cloud, your sins like the morning mist. Return to me, for I have redeemed you" (Isaiah 44:22).

Prayer for Renewal

David's prayer could have ended with verse 9. He had repented. He had trusted God to forgive him.

Nevertheless, he wanted more than just forgiveness for past sins. He wanted to enjoy a full and open relationship with God. He wanted to be the man God wanted him to be. And he knew he could not change himself. Only God could do that.

The emphatic words, "you, you only" in verse 4, were not meant to indicate that David's sinful behavior did not have destructive consequences for other people. Rather, it suggests that he was aware that sin has its origin in the failure to honor God.

In verse 10 he prayed that God would "create" in him a pure heart. This is the same word used in Genesis 1:1, "In the beginning God created the heaven and earth." God's Spirit brooded over the empty darkness and brought forth life. He brought forth beauty and order. That is what the psalmist asked God to do for his heart—to "create" it again, to make it as pure and clean as the newborn earth on the first morning of creation. And that's what God longs to do for us. "I will sprinkle clean water on you, and you will be clean" (Ezekiel 36:25).

The psalmist knew he could not maintain a holy relationship with God on his own. So he prayed for God's Spirit to remain with him and live in him. The Spirit's presence became the focus of his desires. He prayed for a "steadfast spirit" to keep him always rooted in God (v. 10). He prayed for the "Holy Spirit" to live and breathe God's purity within him (v. 11). He prayed for a "willing spirit" to sustain him and keep him walking with God (v. 12).

God's Spirit within us is the only thing that can transform us from weak, self-centered creatures into willing and holy children of the living God. We need His Spirit. Like the psalmist, we need a living, constant relationship with God. That is the focus of all our needs. And that should be the focus of our desires and our prayers.

In the Spirit, we will know the deep joy of salvation (v. 12). It is the joy of being entirely right with God. It is the joy of knowing we are enveloped in His mighty love every moment, now and forever. It is the joy of resting completely in Him.

David's fall into sin and the history of the subsequent monarchy are often very embarrassing. So is the behavior of the disciples in the Gospels (see Matthew 26:56). So is the situation of the Early Church, revealed in the letters of Paul to the Corinthians. So is the history of the Christian church throughout the centuries. So, too, are the details of our life stories, if we are honest enough to admit it. In short, Psalm 51 is not just about David; it is also about us! Failure and sin too often pervade our lives. It is indeed very embarrassing. However, the good news is even more pervasive. Psalm 51 is not just about human nature; it is also about God's nature. The good news is that God is willing to forgive sinners and re-create people! He is even willing and able to keep us from sinning as we allow the sanctifying work of the Holy Spirit to cleanse and purify us completely.

Spiritual Sacrifices

Again, the prayer could have ended after verse 12. David had just experienced the wonderful freedom of forgiveness. He'd prayed for God's Spirit to fill him, keep him, and return to him the full joy of his salvation.

Yet when we've "connected" with God to that degree, how could we possibly stop there? His wonderful Spirit, His peace, joy, and freedom are flowing through us. We want to respond to Him. Walking in His Spirit, we want to do the things Christ would do.

The psalmist first wanted to share God and His wonderful forgiveness with others (v. 13). The more meaningful Christ becomes to us, the more we want everyone else to know Him. Freed from the terrible burden of guilt, David wanted to sing of God's righteousness, that is, His goodness and mercy (v. 14). The desire to praise God is itself a gift from God. It is one of the fruits of His presence within us. The psalmist asked for that gift. "O Lord, open my lips, and my mouth will declare your praise" (v. 15). He wanted to respond to God with all the praise that He deserves. He wanted his life to become a symphony of worship to the One who had forgiven, lifted, and restored him from his sin.

Other offerings, other sacrifices are meaningless without a humble heart and a broken spirit, completely given to God. The Old Testament declares, "For this is what the high and lofty One says—he who lives forever, whose name is holy: 'I live in a high and holy place, but also with him who is contrite and lowly in spirit'" (Isaiah 57:15). The New Testament echoes, "Blessed are the poor in spirit, for theirs is the kingdom of heaven" (Matthew 5:3).

This is what pleases God—a heart that is completely open to Him. He will come and live in that heart.

That is what our Father desires with us—fellowship. He knows that we are weak. "For he knows how we are formed, he remembers that we are dust" (Psalm 103:14).

He knows that our best intentions sometimes waver. Still, He asks one thing—always, only, this one thing—that we trust Him. He asks that we trust Him enough to be open about our failures. He wants us to bring them immediately and honestly to Him, seeking His forgiveness and renewal.

Confession is a wonderful gift of God. If we use it, not even sin need keep us from Him.

Words to Remember: *If we confess our sins, he is faithful and just and will forgive us our sins and purify us from all unrighteousness* (1 John 1:9).

Away in foreign fields they wondered how
  Their simple words had power—
At home the Christians, two or three had met
  To pray an hour.
Yes, we are always wondering, wondering how—
  Because we do not see
Someone—perhaps unknown and far away—
  On bended knee.

—Anonymous

John 17

[1]After Jesus said this, he looked toward heaven and prayed:

"Father, the time has come. Glorify your Son, that your Son may glorify you. [2]For you granted him authority over all people that he might give eternal life to all those you have given him. [3]Now this is eternal life: that they may know you, the only true God, and Jesus Christ, whom you have sent. [4]I have brought you glory on earth by completing the work you gave me to do. [5]And now, Father, glorify me in your presence with the glory I had with you before the world began.

[6]"I have revealed you to those whom you gave me out of the world. They were yours; you gave them to me and they have obeyed your word. [7]Now they know that everything you have given me comes from you. [8]For I gave them the words you gave me and they accepted them. They knew with certainty that I came from you, and they believed that you sent me. [9]I pray for them. I am not praying for the world, but for those you have given me, for they are yours. [10]All I have is yours, and all you have is mine. And glory has come to me through them. [11]I will remain in the world no longer, but they are still in the world, and I am coming to you. Holy Father, protect them by the power of your name— the name you gave me—so that they may be one as we are one. . . .

[20]"My prayer is not for them alone. I pray also for those who will believe in me through their message, [21]that all of them may be one, Father, just as you are in me and I am in you. May they also be in us so that the world may believe that you have sent me. [22]I have given them the glory that you gave me, that they may be one as we are one: [23]I in them and you in me. May they be brought to complete unity to let the world know that you sent me and have loved them even as you have loved me."

CHAPTER 6

The Challenge of Intercessory Prayer

IT IS AN AWESOME THING to be remembered in prayer. To be lifted in prayer by a spouse, family member, friend, or pastor, indicates that our name and circumstance are being brought to the attention of Almighty God. We realize that others are standing with us. We know that we are not alone, that the circumstance is not as dismal as it may seem.

To have the Son of God pray for us is even more incredible. Unlike the capricious Greek and Roman gods, who were even contemptuous toward human beings, Jesus prayed for His followers and for those who would believe through their message. As the Son of God, He demonstrated great interest in and care for humans. To be prayed for by the Son should humble us, for we do not deserve it. Jesus Christ showed us through His prayer that we are not alone in our circumstances.

John 17, the longest recorded prayer of Jesus, comes immediately prior to the first of the events that we normally connect with the Easter story. In fact, the verse that follows the conclusion of this prayer (18:1) says: "When he had finished praying, Jesus left with his disciples and crossed the Kidron Valley. On the other side there was an olive grove [the Garden of Gethsemane], and he and his disciples went into it."

Some believe John 17 took place in an upper room somewhere in Jerusalem. This time of prayer concluded an evening where Jesus and His disciples partook of the Passover meal together, after which Jesus promised them the Holy Spirit, preparing them for His soon departure.

Here, on the eve of arrest, trial, crucifixion, and death, Jesus prayed for His disciples and for those who would believe in the Good News. Jesus was entrusting their future, the future of the covenant community to God. Does this not say something to us? The future of the community of faith is not entrusted to us. Our future is in God's hands. Jesus' final words before the Easter weekend events were not last-minute instructions to the community about what it should do in His absence. Instead, His words turn the future of the community over to God. The Church's future is thus shown to be God's, not ours. The future of the Church ultimately does not depend on or derive from the Church's own work but rests with God.

There is nothing more wonderful, more uplifting, more stabilizing than to hear friends say, "I'm praying for you." It is even more helpful to know that Jesus himself is praying for you and me. His prayer for us did not conclude on the night of His betrayal and arrest. Our Lord "lives forever," having obtained "a permanent priesthood;" and He "always lives to intercede for [us]" (Hebrews 7:24-25).

John 17 gives us a glimpse into the New Testament's "Most Holy Place" (Hebrews 9:8). How fitting that Jesus' final discourse to His disciples would reveal the heart of our mighty Intercessor. This high-priestly prayer, as it has rightly been called, occurred in the hour of His greatest crisis.

Jesus Prays for Himself

The setting of John 17 is an upper room in Jerusalem. Upper rooms in the first century were just that—second or third story rooms. (At least, we know one upper room was on the third floor, the one from which poor Eutychus fell [Acts 20:8]). Usually they were built on the roof of Hebrew homes for privacy, the entertainment of guests, or comfort in the hot season.

Sometimes the upper room was just a tent on the flat roof, but usually it was a regular room. Some were quite large. The one where Jesus celebrated the Passover was large enough to accommodate His final supper with the disciples. The entire Christian community of 120 prayed together in an upper room following His ascension (Acts 1:13-15).

John 17 is an example of what we call intercessory prayer, a type of prayer that lifts up the lives and needs of others. Jesus' prayer began with an address to His Father (v. 1). The intimacy of His relationship to the Father is clear. Jesus spoke confidently to God as we would speak to a friend or parent. His prayer was not an intrusion. The Father was readily accessible.

Jesus announced, "The time has come" (v. 1). He was fully aware that the crucial moment in God's mighty plan of redemption had arrived. The climax of Jesus' earthly life and ministry, His atoning sacrifice for sin, was at hand.

Jesus made only two requests for himself, neither of which was selfish. First, that in this moment of crisis, He would glorify the Father (v. 1). Second, that the Father's glory would be seen in Him (v. 5).

The glory Jesus brought to the Father consisted in giving eternal life to His disciples (v. 2). The mutual glorification of Father and Son was possible because the Father gave Him authority "over all people" (v. 2). Christ's universal authority allowed Him to free all people from sin and give them eternal life.

Jesus defined what that meant. "Now this is eternal life: that they may know you, the only true God, and Jesus Christ, whom you have sent" (v. 3). Eternal life is more than "head knowledge." It is an intimate "heart knowledge." It means joyfully recognizing the Father's sovereignty, accepting His love, and personally experiencing intimate fellowship with Him.

Jesus made a great claim. "I have brought you glory on earth by completing the work you gave me to do" (v. 4). He enjoyed glory with the Father before they laid the foundations of the world (v. 5). Yet, He left that glory to bring glory to His Father here on earth (see Philippians 2:6-7).

The hour had come for restoration to His former glory. Jesus had faithfully accomplished His Father-appointed task. God had given Him authority to grant eternal life. Though Jesus had not yet suffered on the Cross, He knew the outcome and could treat it as having already been done. He was getting ready to return to "the right hand of the Majesty in heaven" (Hebrews 1:3).

Jesus had come from God and soon would return to God. His greatest gift to humanity in the time between those events was the glory of the Cross. That such a painful, disgraceful death should be considered glorious is part of the mystery and majesty of redemption.

In the Old Testament, the high priest was appointed to represent the people before God. He dealt with sins and weaknesses by offering the necessary sacrifices (Hebrews 5:3). However, as a link between God and humans, the Old Testament priest was never enough. He was merely a foreshadow of the coming perfect Intermediary.

Hebrews 4:14 affirms that in Jesus "we have a great high priest." As a human being, He is able to sympathize with us in our weaknesses. Because Jesus was both God and a man, He is an adequate link between the Father and us. So the Scripture says, "Let us then approach the throne of grace with confidence, so that we may receive mercy and find grace to help us in our time of need" (4:16). When we fail and are ashamed, or when we are overwhelmed and need help desperately, we need never draw back. Jesus, human like us, will understand. And Jesus, as God, has the necessary resources to offer aid.

Jesus Prays for His Disciples

Next in John 17, Jesus focused His prayer on the disciples. Jesus was preparing to leave them. Though it brought sadness, the disciples must have been comforted by what they heard.

Jesus revealed the Father (v. 6). He has made it possible for us to see what God is really like. Jesus brought a remote, invisible God so close that even the simplest person can speak to Him, use His name, and come to know Him personally.

The Father gave the disciples to Jesus. Jesus thanked God

for giving them to Him and commended them for their obedience. These men realized that Jesus came from God. They saw God in Jesus. They kept the word of God they heard from Jesus. Eleven disciples, schooled by Jesus for three short years, were enough to change the world. What confidence Jesus had in such a small beginning!

Jesus prayed for the disciples, specifically, that they would be spared the disunity that would tear them apart and keep them from achieving His purpose for them. His prayer was simple and direct: "that they may be one as we are one" (v. 11). Jesus prayed that the disciples would experience unity of purpose, activity, and character as the Father and the Son did within the Godhead. He did not want them to disintegrate into little snarling sects, condemning one another, opposing one another, fighting one another.

Jesus prayed for their protection by the power of the name of the "Holy Father" (v. 11). His power is sufficient to keep them in a wicked world. Jesus asked the Holy Father, whose holiness separates Him from the world, to stand guard over those who are holy and separate in that world.

William Barclay wrote, "It is an uplifting thing to feel that God is the sentinel who stands over our lives to protect us and guard us from the assaults of evil."*

God is guarding, protecting, and keeping. However, the disciples were not fully equipped for their task until they were purified and set apart, receiving the enabling power of the Spirit. Earlier, Jesus had promised to send the Spirit to lead them into all truth (16:13). Before His ascension, Jesus would command them to tarry for power before they went forth to witness (Luke 24:49).

Jesus Prays for All Believers

In the conclusion of His prayer in John 17, Jesus interceded for all who would believe in Him "through [the disciples'] message" (v. 20).

In that statement, Jesus prayed for us. His eyes of faith looked into the distant future to see sons and daughters who would enter the Christian faith. What confident faith and radiant certainty!

Jesus prayed that believers might also be one (v. 21) in the same unity He prayed would characterize His disciples. Of all the things Jesus could have prayed for us, why did He pray for this all-important oneness?

The answer is that disunity is one of the greatest obstacles to a skeptical world. When the world sees divisions, exclusiveness, carnal competition, and disunity, they find it hard to accept the gospel message. Christ's work is hindered. Jesus' prayer is frustrated.

The unity for which Jesus prayed is not an organizational or ecclesiastical unity. Denominations and local churches will never be organized exactly the same way. Modes of worship and doctrinal understandings will differ. Rather, this is a unity of love. Only love can break down the barriers of sectarianism and draw us together within the Body of Christ.

Jesus prayed for unity "so that the world may believe" (v. 21). Believers united in faith and love exert a powerful influence everywhere in the world. When we are torn asunder by strife and dissension, the world ignores our message. The Church is the one place where we have a right to expect the unity of love. It is convincing proof to the world of the truth of Christianity and of the place of Christ.

Jesus also prayed that we might have His glory (v. 22). When believers are in Christ, then Christ is in them. This is the glory that Jesus manifested in three ways:
- through the Cross
- through His perfect obedience to the Father's will
- and through His life, words, and works.

When we believe, we become partakers of all the riches that are in Christ (see Ephesians 1:3 and 2 Peter 1:4). When all the members of the Church everywhere have become partakers of these blessings, the Church, of course, will be one just as the Father and Son are one.

Upon completion of this prayer, Jesus went directly to the events of His betrayal, trial, and crucifixion. This was the last time He taught the disciples before Calvary. How fitting that His last words were not of defeat but of victory, not of gloom but of glory.

A Final Picture

Two ladies lived at a convalescent center. Both were recovering from strokes. Betty had some paralysis on her right side, and Lou's left side was restricted. Each lady was an accomplished pianist, and each was devastated because she could not play the piano.

The therapist sat Betty and Lou at the piano. With a little encouragement, they began playing pieces together, each playing with her healthy hand. The lovely music from two ladies who had felt isolated and obsolete was a great blessing to many. Together, from their functioning parts, one harmonious whole emerged.

Such unity is not only possible but essential in God's kingdom.

*William Barclay, *The Gospel of John*, vol. 2 of *The Daily Study Bible* (Philadelphia: The Westminster Press, 1956), 253.

Words to Remember: *Therefore he is able to save completely those who come to God through him, because he always lives to intercede for them* (Hebrews 7:25).

God's way of answering the Christian's prayer for more patience, experience, hope and love often is to put him into the furnace of affliction.

—Richard Cecil

1 Timothy 2

[1]I urge, then, first of all, that requests, prayers, intercession and thanksgiving be made for everyone— [2]for kings and all those in authority, that we may live peaceful and quiet lives in all godliness and holiness. [3]This is good, and pleases God our Savior, [4]who wants all men to be saved and to come to a knowledge of the truth. [5]For there is one God and one mediator between God and men, the man Christ Jesus, [6]who gave himself as a ransom for all men—the testimony given in its proper time. [7]And for this purpose I was appointed a herald and an apostle—I am telling the truth, I am not lying—and a teacher of the true faith to the Gentiles.

[8]I want men everywhere to lift up holy hands in prayer, without anger or disputing.

Exodus 32

[7]Then the LORD said to Moses, "Go down, because your people, whom you brought up out of Egypt, have become corrupt. [8]They have been quick to turn away from what I commanded them and have made themselves an idol cast in the shape of a calf. They have bowed down to it and sacrificed to it and have said, 'These are your gods, O Israel, who brought you up out of Egypt.'

[9]"I have seen these people," the LORD said to Moses, "and they are a stiff-necked people. [10]Now leave me alone so that my anger may burn against them and that I may destroy them. Then I will make you into a great nation."

[11]But Moses sought the favor of the LORD his God. "O LORD," he said, "why should your anger burn against your people, whom you brought out of Egypt with great power and a mighty hand? [12]Why should the Egyptians say, 'It was with evil intent that he brought them out, to kill them in the mountains and to wipe them off the face of the earth'? Turn from your fierce anger; relent and do not bring disaster on your people. [13]Remember your servants Abraham, Isaac and Israel, to whom you swore by your own self: 'I will make your descendants as numerous as the stars in the sky and I will give your descendants all this land I promised them, and it will be their inheritance forever.'" [14]Then the LORD relented and did not bring on his people the disaster he had threatened. . . .

[30]The next day Moses said to the people, "You have committed a

great sin. But now I will go up to the LORD; perhaps I can make atonement for your sin."

[31]So Moses went back to the LORD and said, "Oh, what a great sin these people have committed! They have made themselves gods of gold. [32]But now, please forgive their sin—but if not, then blot me out of the book you have written."

CHAPTER 7

The Risks and Rewards of Intercession

I REMEMBER WELL what my father said after the last national election. He was unhappy that his candidate had lost. He was extremely unhappy that his candidate's opponent had won. There was no mistaking my father's political agenda; anyone within earshot got an earful. Plain and simple, he didn't like the man who had just been elected president of the United States.

Yet, I also remember something else my father said that seemed odd to some of his likeminded peers. He said, "I may not like the man, but you can rest assured that I will pray for him every day for the next four years."

Praying on behalf of others, sometimes even others who are not like us or we don't personally like, is part of the idea of what we call "intercessory prayer."

Christians have the privilege and responsibility to pray for people other than themselves. They have opportunity to work with the purposes of God in the lives of individuals, both in our immediate community and in the world at large. The influence of intercessory prayer is indeed a powerful resource that we can choose to use for the benefit of others.

Today, there are many people who need our prayers to make it through a particular set of difficult circumstances, to turn from a life of sin, or to make the kinds of decisions that will positively affect many. Right now we have the opportunity to move beyond the limiting boundaries of prayers for our own needs and to become totally involved in the needs of others. In this chapter, we focus on how God's grace is delivered to others through our intercessory prayers. We look at two passages—one from the New Testament and one from the Old. In the New Testament scripture, we encounter the *principles* of intercessory prayer. In the Old Testament verses, we explore a *model* of intercessory prayer.

In Paul's first letter to Timothy, we find guiding principles for "requests, prayers, intercession . . . made for everyone" (1 Timothy 2:1). We are urged to pray for our political leaders regardless of our political preferences. We are to pray for the salvation of all people. And we will see that Paul even suggested what our posture and attitude should be as we pray for others.

From Paul's prayer principles, we move to a look at a real example of the effort required to intercede. As Moses came down the mountain after receiving the Ten Commandments, he found idol worship occurring. The people had built a golden calf while he was away, and they were worshiping this substitute for God.

Moses had the courage to "stand between"—the literal meaning of the word "intercession"—the people and God's displeasure to plead for God's mercy. Moses put his own eternal destiny at risk in behalf of the Israelites to convince God to show them mercy. Moses' example reveals the risks and rewards of intercessory prayer.

We need to understand intercession. We want to gain a clear grasp of what intercession is and how it works. Our responsibility to practice intercession, however, is not dependent upon our thorough understanding of it. The call to intercession is clear, whether we comprehend it all or not. The exercise of prayer—including intercession—is a mystery that is not easily reduced to human analysis. It is a spiritual exercise that unfolds its meaning and power as we practice it. The first lesson about intercession is that we should not wait until we know how to do it right before we do it. If we get started, God will give us some on-the-job training.

Intercession—Labor for the Kingdom

Intercession is entering into the work of the Kingdom through prayer. It is active partnership with God in His work for the sake of His purposes. This may be different from how we have previously thought about intercession. We sometimes approach intercession as if it were an opportunity to present our "shopping list" to God. We come to God with our requests and advice about what needs to be done and even how God should accomplish it. Often we view prayer as an opportunity to review our unrealized agenda of hopes and present our case to God.

Sometimes we approach intercession in the same way my wife and I recently bought a new house. We went through the house with the builder and tried to identify all the things that we wanted corrected. In the same way, we often walk through our lives and bring the problems to God's attention. It is true that God welcomes the sharing of every concern, disappointment, and hope of our lives. However, intercession is less about desiring things *from* God than desiring things *with* God.

Intercession is taking God's work and making it our own, identifying so completely with Christ that we share His burden. It is voluntarily placing ourselves into the "harness" alongside Christ in the labor of the Kingdom.

Paul reflects that value in his call to prayer recorded in 1 Timothy 2. The prayers and intercession "for kings and all those in authority . . . pleases God" (vv. 2-3). Such prayer serves the purpose of God, "who wants all men to be saved and to come to a knowledge of the truth" (v. 4). Praying for national leaders is not about seeking their personal blessing or success. It is about praying that their lives and work might be ordered in such a way as to permit and encourage God's work.

Understanding intercession in this way may help to relieve some of our struggles in praying for political leaders. When we see intercession as requesting God's help in fulfilling *our* agenda, we find it hard to offer "political" prayers. When we pray for leaders with whom we disagree, we are uncomfortable asking for God's blessing for them (that is, for God to help them to realize their agenda). We may feel that the work of those leaders is at cross-purposes with the Kingdom. How can we ask God to bless persons in their work against Him? However, when our concern is about inviting God's will for political leaders, we are interceding for God to accomplish *His* purposes for and through those leaders.

Kingdom intercession will also elevate our intercession for leaders with whom we agree. No matter how noble and right-minded we might feel particular leaders are, their agendas always fall short of God's agenda. When our intercession merely asks for God's blessing on the work of a "good" leader, we have settled for far less than what God desires. Prayer for the godly leader is essentially the same as for the ungodly. We invite *God's* purposes to be accomplished for them and through them. We bring all kinds of leaders equally before the throne of God in prayer. There, we lift our desire that God's will be realized in their exercise of earthly power.

Intercession is a labor in prayer for the work of the Kingdom. It involves identifying so completely with God's will and purposes that we desire what God desires. We share the burden, through prayer, of inviting the realization of God's kingdom.

Learning to Intercede

If intercession is about what God desires, then preparation for such prayer involves *learning* what God desires. Our tendency is to prepare for intercession by reviewing what *we* desire. We identify the areas of our lives that fall short of our hopes and expectations. We determine the things that move us and touch our hearts with hurt or longing. These are the things we bring to God in prayer. However, if intercession is about sharing God's burden and desiring what He desires, then we need to start with God's perspective and God's heart rather than our own.

Our intercession needs to be grounded in a growing knowledge of God's will and an increasing sensitivity to His direction. It will result in greater awareness of what is on God's heart and a deepening burden on our hearts for the same things. As we see things from God's view, our hearts will be moved and broken by the things that move Him.

Paul's understanding of God's agenda shaped his call to prayer. God outlined to Moses the reasons for His anger and disappointment, and this became the basis for Moses' prayer of intercession. Moses interceded on the basis of God's plan in creating and delivering His people. For both Paul and Moses, intercessory prayer was about God's agenda, rather than their own desires.

The Cost of Intercession

There is a cost associated with a ministry of true intercessory prayer. Intercession that is about our concerns and for our benefit usually has little cost. Intercession that shares God's burden demands a price. Moses illustrates that cost in a dramatic way in Exodus 32. He identified so completely with the people of Israel and God's plan for them that he put himself at risk when he prayed: "Oh, what a great sin these people have committed! They have made themselves gods of gold. But now, please forgive their sin—but if not, then blot me out of the book you have written" (vv. 31-32).

He did that despite God's apparent offer to bless him personally after the people would be destroyed. God told Moses, "I have seen these people, . . . and they are a stiff-necked people. Now leave me alone so that my anger may burn against them and that I may destroy them. Then I will make you into a great nation" (vv. 9-10).

Moses set aside his personal interests and assumed the burden of intercession. Moses models the inevitable cost of intercession.

Christ also often expressed the burden of His compassion. He wept over Jerusalem; He was deeply moved by the crowds; He lived surrounded by the needy. His love took Him to the

Cross for each of us. When we are involved in a ministry of intercession, we are willfully sharing Jesus' burden for the lost world. We see through His eyes, feel with His heart, and make His work our own in prayer.

When we make God's work our burden of concern through intercessory prayer, we will be changed. Those changes will affect us beyond the limits of the prayer closet. The process of making God's burdens our own will change how we live. Entering the ministry of intercessory prayer is about letting our hearts be broken with His for a lost world.

Intercession Makes a Difference

If intercession demands a high price, it also returns rich dividends. Simply put, intercessory prayer makes a difference. Paul assumed the effectiveness of intercession in advancing God's purposes. He stated that the result of intercessory prayer would be "that we may live peaceful and quiet lives in all godliness and holiness" (1 Timothy 2:2). Moses demonstrated the decisive difference his intercession made in the history of the Jewish people. It is difficult to understand everything that was taking place in Moses' interchange with God in Exodus 32 and 33. Yet, our lack of resolution of these interpretive questions need not keep us from the clear message that Moses' intercession really mattered.

In ways that we can't completely understand, intercessory prayer can make us effective partners with God in His work. We may be changed personally by intercession, but the change is not limited to us. Prayer is meaningful and productive labor for His entire Kingdom.

Occasionally an elderly saint will say, "About all I can do is pray." Often their tone is apologetic, expressing their regret that they aren't able to do "significant" work in the Kingdom. Such a sentiment fails to appreciate the significance of the ministry of prayer and the power of intercession. It doesn't recognize the "work" character of intercession or its potential impact for the Kingdom. Without intercessory prayer, the Kingdom cannot come.

Words to Remember: *If my people, who are called by my name, will humble themselves and pray and seek my face and turn from their wicked ways, then will I hear from heaven and will forgive their sin and will heal their land* (2 Chronicles 7:14).

God does not listen to the prayers of the proud.

—Hebrew Proverb

1 Kings 8

²²Then Solomon stood before the altar of the LORD in front of the whole assembly of Israel, spread out his hands toward heaven ²³and said:

"O LORD, God of Israel, there is no God like you in heaven above or on earth below—you who keep your covenant of love with your servants who continue wholeheartedly in your way. ²⁴You have kept your promise to your servant David my father; with your mouth you have promised and with your hand you have fulfilled it—as it is today. . . .

⁴⁶"When they sin against you—for there is no one who does not sin—and you become angry with them and give them over to the enemy, who takes them captive to his own land, far away or near; ⁴⁷and if they have a change of heart in the land where they are held captive, and repent and plead with you in the land of their conquerors and say, 'We have sinned, we have done wrong, we have acted wickedly'; ⁴⁸and if they turn back to you with all their heart and soul in the land of their enemies who took them captive, and pray to you toward the land you gave their fathers, toward the city you have chosen and the temple I have built for your Name; ⁴⁹then from heaven, your dwelling place, hear their prayer and their plea, and uphold their cause. ⁵⁰And forgive your people, who have sinned against you; forgive all the offenses they have committed against you, and cause their conquerors to show them mercy; ⁵¹for they are your people and your inheritance, whom you brought out of Egypt, out of that iron-smelting furnace.

⁵²"May your eyes be open to your servant's plea and to the plea of your people Israel, and may you listen to them whenever they cry out to you. ⁵³For you singled them out from all the nations of the world to be your own inheritance, just as you declared through your servant Moses when you, O Sovereign LORD, brought our fathers out of Egypt."

CHAPTER 8

Praying in Public

IT IS IMPORTANT to know why and how we pray personally, but it is also important for us to learn why and how we pray corporately. In public prayer, the words are not directed at the rest of the assembly. The words are directed toward God. The congregation is not simply focused upon the one who is praying. They also look to God in prayer. The one who prays publicly gives an audible voice for the entire congregation. The spoken prayer prompts the listeners in their silent prayers, as we express our unity in the faith. A public prayer is often the way someone in the group can uphold someone else whose faith might be weak at that moment.

Many of us feel anxiety when asked to pray in public. We are helped when we see that public prayers are still personal in nature—personal in that they are conversation directed toward the Lord. We do not need to spout theological superlatives. We do not need to be verbose. We do not need to be eloquent. We simply need to be sincere. In doing so, we will represent the congregation well.

In this chapter, we turn to a close examination of the public prayer King Solomon offered as he dedicated the newly completed temple to the Lord early in his reign. In Solomon's dedication prayer, we see an example of the many functions of public prayer. Community prayers are not simply flowery speeches but are sincere words lifted up in behalf of the whole group. Solomon acted as a leader for the people in praising God and seeking God's will.

Why Pray in Public?

Prayer is a natural part of our relationship with God. It is a personal conversation with an ever-present Friend.

So why should we pray aloud in front of others? Does it make sense? Is it even scriptural?

For many of us, there is no more uncomfortable time in public worship than when we feel we'll be called on to lead in prayer. We've even developed a set of tricks to avoid being asked. When prayer time comes, we look in another direction, as if preoccupied. We look busy, perhaps reading or taking notes. Or we subtly move out of the leader's field of vision by deftly hiding behind the person standing in front of us.

We feel self-conscious about praying aloud. Even worse, we may feel insincere, like we're performing. We might even listen to others and sometimes wonder how much they're praying and how much they're just saying what the crowd wants to hear.

Thinking as a Member of a Community

We are each part of a group of people—a community. In fact, we are members of several communities—such as family, church, city, and nation. We have received much from them. As we mature, the desire grows to leave them a legacy. In a sense, we owe them a debt. We want to give something back to the community that has given so much to us.

We are heirs to so many of the blessings we enjoy: roads, schools, a stable government, knowledge, freedom and, most of all, our Christian faith. We didn't earn any of these. Others left them to us. They were gifts.

We easily forget that we didn't get where we are on our own. Further, we aren't standing here alone. We won't get where we're going detached from others; and when we get there, we won't be there in isolation.

God created us, not just as individuals but as members of a community. We were born into a family, a circle of people, a society. When we are "born again," we become a member of His family, His Body. Our past, present, and future are bound up with this community. It is a major part of our entire existence.

Thus, self-centeredness is foolish. It ignores the reality of community. Self-centeredness fails to face our roots, our debts, and our needs.

We need to think as a member of a community. We need to work and even dream on behalf of the community, and not as an isolated individual. As we do, we can no longer simply pray lonely, selfish prayers.

Praying as a Member of a Community

Solomon stood at the altar of God before a great throng of Israelites. They were there to dedicate the Temple that Solomon had built, a temple where God's name would reside.

Solomon admitted that not even the heavens and the earth could contain the Lord. Given that fact, it seems a bit incredulous to build a temple to house the Lord. If the Lord cannot be confined by all of heaven, He surely cannot fit into a small building. Solomon knew that. For this reason, he said that the Lord's name would dwell there. What does it mean for the Lord's name to be there?

Unlike today, when a name is often viewed as a convenient label, in Solomon's culture, the name of someone or something was an extension of that person or thing. Thus, to say that God's name would dwell within the Temple was to say that God himself would be there. The Temple served as a listening post or sounding board, continually receptive to any prayer directed toward it.

However, the Temple was not Solomon's idea. His father David dreamed of it and planned it. He had gathered materials for its building, and many from all over the country had contributed generously. God had chosen Solomon to build this temple before Solomon knew anything about it. Solomon had inherited the temple project. And further, the Temple was not built primarily for Solomon but for the people of Israel.

When Solomon stood before God to pray a prayer of dedication, he wasn't primarily representing himself. He was representing the entire nation of Israel—past, present, and future.

He led the people in recognizing God for who He was and for His faithfulness to them. He reached back to his father David and saw that what God had promised to him was being fulfilled that very day.

When we gather in God's house, we gather not just as individuals; we gather as God's people. We gather together because of the common bond we have in Christ. We gather as His family to look to our Father and to enjoy fellowship in Him as brothers and sisters. We are "us," not a group of "mes."

And we should pray that way. When we are asked to lead in public prayer, we aren't speaking just as an individual. We are leading the entire congregation to God in prayer. We are representing all the people before God, just as Solomon did.

Yet, God's love and our unity in Him doesn't stop at the walls of our individual churches. This love and unity include all who share His Spirit, all whom He loves. We represent them as well when we pray. Thus, when we pray together as a congregation, our petitions should reach beyond our local gathering. They should present the praise and the concerns of God's broader family.

This kind of prayer is not for public prayer alone. If we have God's love in our hearts, if we realize our unity in the Spirit, we can represent God's people before His throne even as we pray privately. We remember that the Lord's Prayer, the model for our daily prayer, is prayed for "us"—not "me."

Such praying broadens our perspective. It lifts our eyes to see God for who He is, not just a personal friend but also the faithful God of all times and peoples. It reminds us who we are, one member of this large human family. Such prayer reminds us of what He has done, is doing, and will do for all those He loves.

As we pray in Christ as a member of His Body, our prayer will reach beyond personal concerns and the pulling in of a few friends along the way. We can pray as part of Christ's Church everywhere. Such broadened vision helps guide and correct our petitions. It expands our hearts and strengthens our faith as we become aware of God working on a broader scale. We pray and think less selfishly, more in line with His will for us. Thus, we pray more effectively.

God sees us, His Church, as "a chosen people, a royal priesthood, a holy nation, a people belonging to God" (1 Peter 2:9). When we praise and petition God, both privately and publicly, as a nation of priests, we come before Him united as His family, His Body. What a powerful way to pray, think, and live!

Joining Our Prayers Together

In 1 Kings 8:46-51, we hear Solomon assuming the role of priest for the nation. He admitted their sinfulness and acknowledged God's justice in punishing them for their sins. He also pleaded for mercy for them. He asked that God forgive and restore His people when they repent. Further, he represented the nation by reminding God that these are His people, whom He has redeemed by His own hand.

As we read all of Solomon's prayer (vv. 23-53), we hear the sincerity in his words. He had a heart for the people and for God. For him, public prayer was not a performance. It was natural. It was heartfelt. It was meaningful and important.

A test of character is the attitude one takes toward his or her inheritance. It is a matter of honor to keep faith with those who have preceded us in life and death. Solomon therefore closed his dedicatory prayer on a strategic note by reference to Israel's heritage. A college professor once said that the strongest appeal he could make to a wayward student was to remind him or her of parental sacrifices and expectations.

When we have a heart for God and a heart for His people, and remember how we are connected in community, representing others to God in prayer can be a natural activity for us.

Notice one other thing about Solomon's prayer. By praying that God would hear the prayers of His people, Solomon joined his prayers to theirs. He united his prayer with the prayer of all God's people, present and future.

When we pray as a member of God's people, we join our prayers to the prayers of all other members of His family. Such prayer joins God's people in heart and in purpose, aligning them with Christ. When we pray for God's people, we are joining our prayers with those of Christ himself. He is with the Father, now and always, interceding for us.

When we ask as a united community, we establish a faith relationship with God. We align ourselves with Him and His heart, His purpose, and His whole history of mighty acts of salvation. We make ourselves dependent on Him. Resting in Him completely, we are in a position of unlimited power and unshakable security. "If you remain in me and my words remain in you, ask whatever you wish, and it will be given you" (John 15:7).

The next time you're in church, look around. Take note of all the people God has created. See them in their variety, their potential, and their need. Then when the time comes to pray, lift them to God our Father. Come before Him as part of the group, whether you're leading in prayer or not.

Words to Remember: *Hear the supplication of your servant and of your people Israel when they pray toward this place. Hear from heaven, your dwelling place, and when you hear, forgive* (1 Kings 8:30).

A man ought to know when to pray. It's pretty late to pray for oars when the boat's on the brink of the falls.　　　　　　　　—The Country Parson

Psalm 25

¹To you, O Lord, I lift up my soul;
  ²in you I trust, O my God.
Do not let me be put to shame,
  nor let my enemies triumph over me.
³No one whose hope is in you
  will ever be put to shame,
but they will be put to shame
  who are treacherous without excuse.

⁴Show me your ways, O Lord,
  teach me your paths;
⁵guide me in your truth and teach me,
  for you are God my Savior,
  and my hope is in you all day long.
⁶Remember, O Lord, your great mercy and love,
  for they are from of old.
⁷Remember not the sins of my youth
  and my rebellious ways;
according to your love remember me,
  for you are good, O Lord.

⁸Good and upright is the Lord;
  therefore he instructs sinners in his ways.
⁹He guides the humble in what is right
  and teaches them his way.
¹⁰All the ways of the Lord are loving and faithful
  for those who keep the demands of his covenant.

James 1

⁵If any of you lacks wisdom, he should ask God, who gives gener-ously to all without finding fault, and it will be given to him. ⁶But when he asks, he must believe and not doubt, because he who doubts is like a wave of the sea, blown and tossed by the wind. ⁷That man should not think he will receive anything from the Lord.

CHAPTER 9

Praying for God's Guidance

EVERY DAY we make dozens, perhaps hundreds, of decisions. We must decide all kinds of things, from the trivial to the essential. We have to decide what time to get up, what clothes to wear, and what to eat for breakfast. We have to think about how to spend free time, what to buy at the store, or who to visit. We have to choose what attitudes we will allow to focus our thoughts, how we will respond to an unkind word, and how we will resist temptations. Every day we are bombarded with choices—small and large—that call for decisions. Even refusing to make a choice is a decision!

The non-Christian must make those decisions alone, asking each time, "What is *my* best course of action? What will bring *me* the greatest happiness?" However, a Christian, knowing that he or she has a wise and loving Heavenly Father who cares about the direction of his or her life, asks a different question: "What is God's will for me in this situation? How can I please God with my decisions?" The Christian knows that he or she does not have to make decisions in a vacuum; God is there to guide.

Discovering how to make wise, godly decisions is not always as easy as we sometimes make it out to be. There are times when we make bad decisions—sometimes purposely, often mistakenly. We need to be reminded that, through prayer, God is able to direct our paths toward righteousness.

The guidance that we seek from God through prayer does not simply benefit the individual Christian who prays. Though the personal benefit of God's guidance is a tremendous help to us as we try to live good lives, the cumulative effect of individuals of faith being guided by God has a great impact on the whole Body of Christ. The individual believer is part of a community of faith that also seeks to do God's will. So prayers for guidance, though voiced by individuals within the community, eventually bring good to the entire group.

In this chapter, we look at two diverse writers who share something very important. They both know that God is the true source of wisdom and He is willing to share His wisdom with us.

We will look closely at Psalm 25 where the psalmist demonstrated the proper attitude toward God: We should seek wisdom from God because of His goodness and wisdom. We should orient all our efforts around the task of seeking God's direction for our lives. Nothing else is more important.

In the New Testament, we find that James shared the psalmist's attitude toward the greatness of God. However, James was direct and practical in his approach. In essence, he said to us, "God has all the wisdom. Ask him!" James even went a step further by addressing the point that weakens many Christians' prayers. In short, he said, "Ask God, but don't doubt He will answer."

The perspectives of both the psalmist and James are important reminders for us as we are faced daily with choices that require God's wisdom.

Drawn to Prayer

Our Heavenly Father draws us to prayer. He desires a personal relationship with us. He actively seeks it. He nurtures it at every opportunity. He longs for us to turn to Him throughout the day. He wants us to bring Him each need, each failure, and each concern. When life goes well, He wants us to realize that He is blessing us and thank Him for it. When times are difficult, He wants us to trust Him. He wants us to put our whole weight on Him.

What about when we need guidance? What does our Father expect of us then? He knows we're blind when it comes to our ability to see the future. He knows selfish desires and temporary concerns easily sway us. When we need wisdom and guidance, He wants us to turn to Him.

Still, we have important questions. How can we find His guidance? How can we know His will for us? How will we recognize His voice when we hear it?

Many of us have reached points of decision in our lives and have struggled with those questions. Many successful people have acknowledged in their memoirs that whenever they came to an impasse in their work and were completely baffled, they sought wisdom from the Lord.

This was true in the life of the inventor of the telegraph, Samuel F. B. Morse. In an interview, someone inquired, "Professor Morse, when you were making your experiments at the university, did you ever come to a standstill, not knowing what to do next?"

"I've never discussed this with anyone, so the public knows nothing about it. But now that you ask me, I'll tell you frankly—I prayed for more light."

"And did God give you the wisdom and knowledge you needed?" the reporter continued.

"Yes, He did," said Morse. "That's why I never felt I deserved the honors that came to me for the invention associated with my name. I had made a valuable application of the use of electrical power, but it was all through God's help. It wasn't because I was superior to other scientists. When the Lord wanted to bestow this gift on mankind, He had to use someone. I'm just grateful He chose to reveal it to me."

In view of this attitude, it's not surprising that the inventor's first message over the telegraph was "What hath God wrought?"

Every time we face a perplexing problem, we can seek wisdom from God. When the answer comes, we should thank God and give Him all the glory.

Relying on God in Our Need

We need to remember that God is not a computer. When we want immediate relief from temporary pain, we don't punch in the proper code, then expect Him to automatically give us the desired response. He is a living Being. He interacts with us in a living, personal way.

He desires to bless us more deeply and more permanently than we can imagine. He wants us to share His life, His happiness, and His peace. His thoughts are higher than our thoughts. His love is wiser than our requests.

Thus, as we study how to seek God's guidance, we can't look for a step-by-step formula. There are no shortcuts to getting what we want. Instead, we have to try to understand God's ways and to learn to relate to Him as our Father.

This is what we see in the spirit of the psalmist as he turned to God in his need. The opening phrase of Psalm 25 is a moving one. "To you, O LORD, I lift up my soul." I can picture the psalmist standing before God. Looking up, with both hands raised, he was lifting his entire life to God in total dependence. As he did so, we hear in his voice the same anxiety and desperation that we experience when we're in need.

However, we also hear him take a determined step of trust. "In you I trust, O my God" (v. 2). He remembered God's faithfulness in the past. He recalled His reliability. In the midst of threats swirling around him, he consciously took his stand on God's faithfulness. By this step of utter dependence, he stated his trust that the God who had always been faithful would continue to be faithful.

He was not begging for a personal favor. He was not racing into a quick fix so that he could be on his way in a jiffy. Rather, he trusted his whole life to God. He acted in the confidence that God would do what is right. He was relying on God's character.

When troubles are threatening us, when we desperately

need God's guidance and help, we should stop and remember. Remember how much He loves us. Remember His faithfulness through every trial, every circumstance, every need. Remember that God is still the sovereign One.

Then we should put our entire lives into His hands. Stand before Him and lift our whole being to Him. Trust Him. Almighty God will always be our Father. His love will never change. It will never fail.

Trusting God to guide us is the best decision we can ever make. "No one whose hope is in you will ever be put to shame" (v. 3).

Praying for Guidance

Notice that the psalmist didn't pray, "God, just tell me what to do in this situation, and I'll be on my way." He asked to know God's "ways," His "paths" (v. 4). He was talking about a learning process.

God's leading doesn't start and stop at a single critical decision. He doesn't just step in at one turning point and then disappear. Seeking and following God is a daily need, a constant lifestyle. Each day is an unknown, full of unforeseen challenges and opportunities. We need His guidance every day. If we seek and follow Him day by day, we will naturally follow Him through times of major decisions as well. We have an established relationship with Him. We recognize His prompting. We trust the Spirit and follow Him.

If a blind man needed to get to a place he'd never been, how would we guide him? Would we tell him, "Go to the third traffic light, turn left, watch for the convenience store, then . . ."? Not likely. We'd take him by the arm and walk with him. There would be no need to verbalize directions ahead of time. We'd just ask that he trust us and walk with us, step by step.

Our Heavenly Father leads us the same way. He doesn't tell us where to go; He takes us there. He walks with us day by day, step-by-step. He only asks that we trust Him and keep on walking.

A Time of Reflection

One of the good things about experiencing need is that it causes us to come before God. In desperation, we pour out our concerns before Him.

Yet, standing in His presence, we eventually become aware of a deeper need. We somehow sense that we cannot storm into His presence and ask from purely selfish motives. If we come before Him, we come as His children, His servants. We must bow before Him. We must come seeking His will, not our own.

Specifically, if we come seeking guidance, we can't honestly do so without committing ourselves to following Him. Such a commitment involves humbling ourselves. It involves wanting only what He wants. It involves lining ourselves up with Him and His will.

Thus times of need often become times of self-examination and recommitment. In the light of His face, we see ourselves. We see our weakness, our imperfection, our inconsistency. We realize our utter dependence on His love and mercy.

At that point of humility and submission, we can cling to God alone. He is good and upright, and He will instruct us in His way. He will guide the humble into what is right.

Praise His name, He does bless the undeserving! He is merciful, always and forever. No matter how unworthy we are, He always has our best interests at heart. All His ways are loving and faithful.

Still, we must remember that His ways are only loving and faithful for those who follow them. If we disobey—whether from selfishness, fear, or lack of faith—we walk out of His way. We exclude ourselves from His blessings and choose the way of death instead.

God will speak. We must listen. We must follow.

Still, does the wise father guide his child by formulating a plan that covers every detail of the child's life and then reveal that plan step-by-step as each decision must be made? The father who is truly wise teaches his child the basic principles of life. He teaches what is right and wrong, what is wise and what is foolish. He then seeks to train the child to make his or her own decisions, making proper use of those correct guidelines. Such a father is overjoyed when he knows that the child has matured to the point where he or she is able to function independently as an adult and make wise decisions.

If our development of this image of father is correct, how does this example relate to God and His guidance? Does He guide us by laying out a specific plan for our lives step by step? Or does He give increasing freedom and responsibility to Christians in their decision making?

Interestingly, we note that God, as He is revealed from the Old to the New Testament, moves from a highly structured system of regulations governing a wide range of specific behaviors to a system where behavior is to be determined by principles and a personal relationship with God. There was progress from law to Christ, from the bondage of close, restrictive supervision appropriate to immature and willful children to the freedom of responsible adulthood.

Wisdom Is Always Available

God gives His wisdom generously—literally, "simply." He gives it graciously, with an open hand, without any scolding or finding fault. All He asks is that we trust Him.

What a wonderful Father!

Yet, the news gets even better. God gives His wisdom through His Holy Spirit within us, "the Spirit of truth [who] will guide [us] into all truth" (John 16:13). His Spirit doesn't just impart information. He doesn't just change our minds; He changes our hearts. He guides and shapes our thoughts, our emotions, and our reactions. He reshapes us from the inside.

In James 3:13-18, we see the contrast between "wisdom" that "is earthly, unspiritual, of the devil" (v. 15) and God's wisdom. His is a living wisdom that flows from His living presence in our hearts. His wisdom is not just information. It is power. It is inner strength. "The wisdom that comes from heaven" (v. 17) doesn't just help us *think* more like God; it enables us to *act* more like Him. His wisdom is love. His wisdom is gentleness. His wisdom is "pure, then peace-loving, considerate, submissive, full of mercy and good fruit" (v. 17).

Heavenly wisdom is always available to us. All we need to do is heed the scripture, "If any of you lacks wisdom, he should ask God, . . . and it will be given to him" (1:5).

Words to Remember: *Show me your ways, O LORD, teach me your paths; guide me in your truth and teach me, for you are God my Savior, and my hope is in you all day long* (Psalm 25:4-5).

Beware in your prayer, above everything, of limiting God, not only by unbelief, but by fancying that you know what He can do.   —Andrew Murray

James 5

[13]Is any one of you in trouble? He should pray. Is anyone happy? Let him sing songs of praise. [14]Is any one of you sick? He should call the elders of the church to pray over him and anoint him with oil in the name of the Lord. [15]And the prayer offered in faith will make the sick person well; the Lord will raise him up. If he has sinned, he will be forgiven. [16]Therefore confess your sins to each other and pray for each other so that you may be healed. The prayer of a righteous man is powerful and effective.

[17]Elijah was a man just like us. He prayed earnestly that it would not rain, and it did not rain on the land for three and a half years. [18]Again he prayed, and the heavens gave rain, and the earth produced its crops.

2 Corinthians 12

[7]To keep me from becoming conceited because of these surpassingly great revelations, there was given me a thorn in my flesh, a messenger of Satan, to torment me. [8]Three times I pleaded with the Lord to take it away from me. [9]But he said to me, "My grace is sufficient for you, for my power is made perfect in weakness." Therefore I will boast all the more gladly about my weaknesses, so that Christ's power may rest on me. [10]That is why, for Christ's sake, I delight in weaknesses, in insults, in hardships, in persecutions, in difficulties. For when I am weak, then I am strong.

CHAPTER 10

Prayer and Healing

YESTERDAY I STAYED IN BED all day. No, it wasn't a holiday; and, no, I'm not just naturally lazy. I had a cold—a really bad cold. Stuffy nose, watery eyes, chills, fever, and aches in every joint in my body. No position felt comfortable. You know the feeling, a general "I don't feel like getting out of bed today." And I didn't.

Sickness, whether a 24-hour flu bug or a life-threatening bout with cancer, can bring out the worst in us. We don't like to be sick. It puts us in a vulnerable position. We often don't have the resources to fight our illnesses alone and must depend on the skills and knowledge of others to help us. Sometimes no one knows what to do, and we are left alone to face our sickness.

Probably no other area of life has solicited as many prayers to God than the prayer for healing. Yet, we have questions. Does God care about our "aches and pain"? Does He care that we suffer? People ask these questions every day. Someone (maybe you) is struggling right now with how to pray for healing, personally or for a loved one. He or she needs and desperately wants to hear today from the God who formed our bodies and cares about our lives.

Different Opinions

They couldn't have been more different. Faced with the serious illness of a loved one, they responded in nearly opposite ways. One went to earnest prayer in full confidence of a positive response, even demanding that God act in the desired way. The other, anxious not to act inappropriately and concerned about praying in the wrong way, was reluctant to pray specifically about the illness at all.

Both of these people were trying to do what they thought was right. Their widely different approaches reflect our own lack of clear understanding of prayer for the sick. In this chapter, we want to understand better how we should pray about sickness.

Come Continually

Let's first try to place prayer for the sick in the right perspective. James suggested we should respond to sickness in the same way as we respond to all of life's experiences. We ought to make it a matter of prayer. Sickness is simply another example of how all of life comes under God's lordship. Trouble and joy, success and sickness all belong in our conversation with God. Prayer is about bringing God's perspective into our life experience and inviting His lordship over both the experience and our response to it. When we bring concerns to God in prayer we are saying, "Lord, bring this matter into focus from your perspective. We invite you to order the situation—and me—according to your will."

We sometimes treat prayer as if it were a sort of divine 911 call. We use it when there's an emergency or when we need something important done. Prayer is left unexpressed until needed. We treat God like the crusty husband treated his wife. She asked him why he never told her he loved her. His reply was that he had told her he loved her 40 years ago when they were married. If anything changed, he would let her know. If we need God, we'll let Him know.

Still, every aspect of our lives belongs, naturally, in our

practice of prayer. So, of course, does the matter of illness. Is anyone sick? Let's make it a matter of prayer!

Just as prayer should be an important part of our individual lives, it should also be a regular part of the life of the Body of Believers we know as the Church. James placed the special prayer for the sick in the community of believers. Call the elders. Gather the righteous to prayer. The prayer life of the Church ought to be continual, bringing the life of the community into God's presence and inviting His perspective. That includes prayer for the sick. On the other hand, we ought to be praying together about more than this week's sick list. Prayer ought to be an important part of the fabric of the life of the community of God's people—including sickness.

Come Boldly

Prayer for healing should come out of a lifestyle of prayer that involves all of life. It also stands on a foundation of our belief in God's character and His power. His character assures us of His welcome to our requests. We know that He cares about every aspect of our lives. We have a standing invitation to speak directly to Him about anything.

We know that God's power is greater than any problem or challenge we can bring to Him. He will never respond, "That's more than I can handle." We know that God is more than able to help us.

God's character and His power help us to come boldly, as Hebrews 4:16 tells us. Knowing that no problem is too great and that His love for us is absolute, we can come before Him with boldness. Even severe sickness that leads to death is not beyond Him. Sin, which leads to eternal death, is not beyond Him. Bring them boldly to the Lord in prayer.

Come Humbly

James specifically included confession in the practice of prayer. Confession is more than a necessary preparation for answered prayer. It is not just part of the method of prayer. Confession brings us into the right perspective for prayer. In

God's presence, we confess our broken humanity. Confession includes willful sin, but it also includes admitting our weaknesses and mistakes before God. Confession recognizes that our holiness, wisdom, and understanding are revealed as meager in His presence. Even the practice of kneeling in prayer is a physical demonstration of our confession of inadequacy in the presence of His perfection.

An enthusiastic young believer criticized prayer that used the tag "according to God's will." "We should be bold," he contended. "We can claim the biblical promises and ask God to do what we want Him to do. Being meekly resigned to God's will fails to exercise the power available to us."

He was probably correct that we should be bold in prayer. On the other hand, his approach to prayer was missing the perspective of confession. Prayer that is brought into focus through confession will be slow to override God's judgment. Confession reminds us that God's agenda is often not the same as ours. It also makes clear to us that His agenda is always infinitely superior to our own.

A popular song of a few years ago described a young man who prayed for the love of a certain girl. He found his love returned and saw this as an answer to his prayer. However, as time went by, he discovered that his beloved was not what he thought. He came to regret the granting of his earlier prayer request. The refrain of the ballad cautioned us to be careful what we pray for, because we might get it.

This song reflects in a humorous way the folly of our limited wisdom. The more serious message cautions us about claiming we know what is best. Prayer conditioned by a healthy dose of confession helps us keep a right perspective, coming humbly to God.

Come Confidently

As James made clear, prayer and faith go hand in hand. Faith is more than an enthusiastic confidence that God will do what we want Him to do. If confession brings us into the right perspective, faith brings the right perspective about God. The primary focus of that belief is not on what God can do but who He is. God's power is important, but His character determines how that power is exercised. Our faith in God's love gives us confidence that He will exercise His power for our benefit.

Prayer that is shaped by faith is confident that God will act for our good. The confidence is not that God will always do what we ask but that He will always do what is for our best.

That confidence is challenged when our trusting prayer is not followed by a positive answer we can recognize. This is true, not only because we are personally disappointed but also because Scripture itself seems to give contradictory answers. James 5 declared that prayer offered in faith would result in healing. "The Lord will lift him up" (v. 15). The next verse reminds us that "the prayer of a righteous man is powerful and effective" (v. 16). On the other hand, 2 Corinthians 12:7-10 tells us that Paul (certainly a righteous man) prayed for relief and didn't receive it. Yet, rather than being disillusioned, he found spiritual victory in the apparently unanswered prayer. Our own experience often reflects this seeming contradiction.

The starting point of our confidence in prayer must be in the character of God. We know the kind of God we serve and worship. We know that He loves us and is always at work for our good. That is, our starting point must always be who God is, not what we see in our circumstances. When we begin by looking at situations, trying to discern in them whether good is at work or not, we are already on the wrong track. For one thing, that approach assumes we will recognize good if we see it. My own experience has repeatedly shown my judgment to be limited and inaccurate. Our faith allows us to begin with the assurance that God is about the business of lifting people up.

Since that is so, we have to assume that appearances to the contrary are misleading and false. That is the lesson that Paul shared in 2 Corinthians 12:7-10. "I thought I knew what was best," he said, in effect, "but God knew better. And I have learned that He was right. So much so," he concluded, "that I now boast and delight in circumstances from which I earlier sought escape." "Boast" (v. 9) and "delight" (v. 10) are pretty strong words! Paul had learned that God is always at work for our good (in fact, for our best) and any perceptions that indicate otherwise are mistaken.

When we seek healing and relief from illness, we should remember that God's vision for those remedies is greater than ours. We think in terms of immediate physical healing and relief. God considers the issue from the perspective of eternity, as well as the complete redemption and transformation of the human person. To demand that God operate on our terms is to limit Him and compromise His best for us.

We expect our doctors to consider our immediate pain in the context of a holistic concern for our health. He or she may determine that some discomfort in the short term is in our best interest. Surgery and chemotherapy, for example, inflict greater suffering in the present in hope of better health in the future. We would think poorly of a doctor who answered our request for immediate relief at the expense of our future health. In fact, we would probably sue a doctor for malpractice if he or she did that—even if it were at our request! Isn't it curious that we are willing to grant physicians a liberty we are often reluctant to grant our Heavenly Father?

As Paul discovered, our witness is powerfully revealed in an active faith that goes beyond our circumstances. How appropriate that it should. Human confidence understands faith that is supported by immediate experience. Faith that rests on circumstances is a fragile faith. The world already has that kind of faith. What humans need is a faith that goes beyond the evidence of experience and remains confident in hope, a faith that is only found through Christ.

Words to Remember: *And the prayer offered in faith will make the sick person well; the Lord will raise him up. If he has sinned, he will be forgiven* (James 5:15).

God is not a cosmic bellboy for whom we can press a button to get things.

—Harry Emerson Fosdick

Habakkuk 1

¹The oracle that Habakkuk the prophet received.

²How long, O Lᴏʀᴅ, must I call for help,
    but you do not listen?
Or cry out to you, "Violence!"
    but you do not save?
³Why do you make me look at injustice?
    Why do you tolerate wrong?
Destruction and violence are before me;
    there is strife, and conflict abounds.
⁴Therefore the law is paralyzed,
    and justice never prevails.
The wicked hem in the righteous,
    so that justice is perverted.

Habakkuk 3

¹A prayer of Habakkuk the prophet. On *shigionoth*.

²Lᴏʀᴅ, I have heard of your fame;
    I stand in awe of your deeds, O Lᴏʀᴅ.
Renew them in our day,
    in our time make them known;
    in wrath remember mercy. . . .

¹⁶I heard and my heart pounded,
    my lips quivered at the sound;
decay crept into my bones,
    and my legs trembled.
Yet I will wait patiently for the day of calamity
    to come on the nation invading us.
¹⁷Though the fig tree does not bud
    and there are no grapes on the vines,
though the olive crop fails
    and the fields produce no food,
though there are no sheep in the pen
    and no cattle in the stalls,
¹⁸yet I will rejoice in the Lᴏʀᴅ,
    I will be joyful in God my Savior.
¹⁹The Sovereign Lᴏʀᴅ is my strength;
    he makes my feet like the feet of a deer,
        he enables me to go on the heights.

CHAPTER 11

Has God Disappointed You?

WRITER M. SCOTT PECK began his best-seller book, *The Road Less Traveled,* with this profound little sentence: "Life is hard."

Life is filled with many kinds of events and experiences. Some we look forward to with great anticipation; others we dread. Some elicit feelings of happiness, thankfulness, and fulfillment; others lead us to anguish, suffering, and disappointment.

Somehow the notion has been passed along that if things are right between God and us, nothing bad will happen. When something undesirable does occur, we conclude that either things are not right with God or that God doesn't care. These notions are faulty. There are certain guarantees in life: joy *and* pain, fulfillment *and* disappointment, restoration *and* suffering. The events of life are not foolproof signs of God's favor or disapproval.

This is one of those chapters that is aptly described by the phrase, "This is where the rubber meets the road!" Life is filled with experiences and events that may cause suffering, anguish, and grief. We cannot avoid these experiences. What we can avoid is the conclusion that *because* these events have occurred *then* God must not care or He must be absent. The occurrence of bad things does not mean that God has left us. Rather, the truth of the gospel is that God has cast His lot with us *despite* the difficulty of life. God may or may not act to radically change the circumstances; however, we can count on the fact that God cares, that He is present, and that He is involved.

Yet, disappointment with God is a stumbling block for many. It is a common experience but not one that many Christians are willing to admit. Disappointment leads to doubt, and doubt does not seem to be a part of genuine faith for many people.

In this chapter, we will confront disappointment head-on by looking at a dialogue between the prophet Habakkuk and God. Habakkuk felt pretty overwhelmed at what was happening in Israel during his time. He couldn't understand why God was handling the situation in the way He was. He couldn't comprehend God's strange method of dealing with the people. In fact, he was outright disappointed that God was using a nation more wicked than the wayward Jews to punish Israel.

We will see how much we are like Habakkuk. We will look into the details of the conversation between Habakkuk and God to discover how our disappointments arise from our feelings of unjustness. We will see how open God is to listening to our complaints and reminding us of His watchful love over us. And, hopefully, we will find a renewed sense of trust and joy in God in the face of our difficulties.

Our Experience with Disappointment

He is one of the finest men I have ever known. He is a person of integrity and competence, compassion and realism. His commitment to God and to the church has long been exemplary. He is, in short, a man deserving of blessing and success. Yet, while his ministry as a layleader in the church has prospered, his secular business has enjoyed only marginal success. At the same time, I have watched others around him. Other persons in his profession who displayed questionable integrity and tainted ethics have prospered. Despite his faithful service and continued prayer for God's help, God doesn't seem to be answering. Why?

"Why" is a question that Habakkuk asked too. Probably all of us can relate to the frustration and disappointment that

Habakkuk expressed. It is the result of our distress when our experience of the world seems out of proper order. It is our response to the contrast between what *should be* and what *is*. The righteous suffer while the wicked prosper. The evildoers go unpunished while the good go unrewarded. It just doesn't seem right. "The law is paralyzed, and justice never prevails" (1:4).

To make matters worse, the problem often remains unresolved even after we have brought it to the Lord's attention. We pray and wait. Still, God does not act to right the wrong. In fact, there are times when the wrong just gets worse. The faithful suffer while those who defy God enjoy prosperity and health. We wonder where God is. "How long, O LORD, must I call for help, but you do not listen?" (1:2).

Habakkuk was not the first to raise the question, "How long?" Many years before Habakkuk had begun his struggle with the problem of the prevalence of evil, oppression, and injustice, the God of grace had asked "How long?" when Israel ignored the goodness involved in His granting a double portion of manna on the day before the Sabbath (Exodus 16:28). When the people showed their unbelief by accepting the report of the skeptical spies, the Lord had asked "How long?" (Numbers 14:11). Without doubt the Lord entered sympathetically into the agonies of His prophet.

In our frustration and disappointment, we cry out, "Why?" How should we understand these experiences? How can we deal with our disappointment? Scripture can help us as we look at the experience of Habakkuk. He lived a long time ago, but he struggled with the same problems. Let's see what his experience can teach us.

Bringing Our Experience to God

The first lesson Habakkuk teaches us is that we can, and should, bring our disappointment and frustration to God. Habakkuk was watching political and military events of his time (around 605 B.C.) with concern. The Assyrian Empire had collapsed, but the Babylonians were assuming power. Judah would soon attract their attention. The results would be catastrophic. Within 20 years, the land would be devastated and the nation destroyed. Judah would cease to exist as a nation. Habakkuk, looking at the horizon of historical developments, saw tragedy and suffering ahead for his people.

It might have been understandable if Judah had abandoned God. Perhaps then we could see the coming destruction as deserved punishment. The confusing reality is that Judah had just undergone national revival. Under King Josiah, the people had been called back to the true worship of Yahweh. (See 2 Kings 22—23 and 2 Chronicles 34—35.) The people had just turned back to God. How could God allow His own people to be overcome by the ruthless Babylonians now?

Habakkuk is strikingly frank and refreshingly bold as he opens his heart to God. Apparently, that's OK. God is not easily offended or frail. He can handle our honesty. That doesn't mean we should curse God or insult Him. It does means we can really open our hearts and share how we feel and what we think. God can handle it.

If we keep our disappointment to ourselves while keeping our conversation with God properly pious, we are headed for trouble. Repression and denial are not Christian strategies for personal problem solving. They are unhealthy and unnecessary. We don't need to hide from problems or difficult issues. There is nothing virtuous about pretending everything is all right when it isn't. Let God in on it. God can not only handle our honesty; He can handle our problems too.

When we keep our feelings of disappointment and frustration to ourselves, we are saying that we can handle them ourselves. We are trying to resolve them on our own terms. *We* want to somehow make them right. Bringing them to God, as Habakkuk did, invites God's resolution on *His* terms. That's not always as easy as we might think. Sometimes we would rather harbor our sense of injustice because we're not ready to invite God into the problem. He may see it differently. He may not affirm our opinions or share our indignation. We would rather interpret the injustice. We want to keep our "spin" on the problem.

Habakkuk made his case while bringing the whole problem to God. He openly shared with God what was on his heart. When he did that, he invited God into the problem. He gave God a chance to show him the view from God's perspective. He allowed God to deal with the injustice on *His* terms. When we bring our experience to God, we are also bringing God into our experience. That's where hope begins.

Bringing Our Judgments to God

When we bring our experience to God, we find that we are also bringing our judgments to God. That is often a disturbing experience. Our assessments and judgments concerning justice and fairness seem so clear and undeniable to us. Yet, when we make our case to God, we find that our judgment isn't always as certain as we think. That's probably one of the reasons we keep our disappointments to ourselves. God's conclusions may not be the same as ours.

A few years ago, a prominent sports figure announced that he had AIDS. He acknowledged that he had engaged in a pattern of high-risk sexual encounters. Nevertheless, he said he couldn't understand why he got AIDS. He concluded that God had chosen him to contract AIDS for a special, divine purpose.

We'll have to "call a foul" on his reasoning. I am sympathetic to his illness and to his struggle to make sense out of his situation. However, I am not impressed with his theology. He contracted AIDS because of the choices *he* made, not the ones God made. His disease was a tragic and unfortunate consequence of his own behavior.

Sometimes our judgments of injustice are similarly flawed. We begin with an inaccurate assessment of our own innocence or someone else's guilt. Sometimes that is true. Still, many times the difficulties we struggle with are, at least in part, of our own making. The bias of our judgments can prevent us from dealing with the things for which we are responsible.

Our judgments are limited and flawed. They are flawed because *we* make them, and *we* are flawed. They are limited because our understanding and knowledge are limited. Our perspective for judgment is influenced and restricted by our experience, feelings, prejudices, and partiality—all the factors that make up our flawed humanity. When we keep our judgment to ourselves, we find it keenly persuasive and convincing. In God's presence, however, we see clearly how our judgment is lacking. It is an uncomfortable but redemptive corrective. God helps us to see our world the way it really is.

Bringing God's Perspective into Focus

In chapter 3, Habakkuk's prayer brought his situation into focus from God's perspective. Remembering God's character and his past actions helped Habakkuk face his current difficulties. He recounted God's works in nature and in history. Remembering what God does and what He is like encouraged him. God has demonstrated throughout history that He is reliable and faithful. His judgment has been consistent and true. While human judgments are persistently revealed as flawed, God's judgments are invariably confirmed as true and right. Seeing his situation from God's perspective filled Habakkuk with awe. "LORD, I have heard of your fame; I stand in awe of your deeds" (v. 2). And it brought a transforming focus. "I heard and my heart pounded . . . and my legs trembled. Yet I will wait patiently for the day of calamity to come on the nation invading us" (v. 16).

Can you remember some times in your life when you were disappointed with God and frustrated with the course of events? You felt distress with what God was doing or not doing. As those situations were eventually resolved, did you discover that your judgments were correct or that God had been right all along?

Not every experience will be clear, and there are some we will never understand in this life. Yet, my experience has consistently confirmed God's judgment. In fact, I am embarrassed to remember how many times I have been frustrated and impatient with God while He was working on a blessing beyond what I could see.

In Scripture and in our own history, we encounter a God

who is consistently faithful and absolutely reliable. His past performance serves as a guarantee of His future conduct. We know what we can expect. We may be a little anxious. Habakkuk vividly described his own trembling, but we can have the same confidence as Habakkuk that God is faithful.

Our Resting Place

Despite Habakkuk's very real concerns and his perceptions of injustice, he found a resting place for his faith. "Though the fig tree does not bud and there are no grapes on the vines, though the olive crop fails and the fields produce no food, though there are no sheep in the pen and no cattle in the stalls, yet I will rejoice in the LORD, I will be joyful in God my Savior" (3:17-18).

In these verses, Habakkuk declared a place of trust that is beyond the reach of circumstances. It cannot be contradicted by our perceptions. It is a place of faith that doesn't rest on what we see or know but on the character of God. We may not understand circumstances, but we know God's character. It may not be clear at the moment what God is doing, but we know how God works. Beyond our understanding or experience, we can trust God. He is faithful and worthy of our trust.

Only those who rest their trust in the character of God can find the resting place Habakkuk described. It is a faith that is hopeful and confident even in the midst of distressing circumstances. Our worldly affairs may lie in ruin. Our best efforts may remain unrewarded. Injustice may reign as far as our eyes can see. Still, we will trust the One who works beyond where we can see. The Lord is our strength. He is taking us to the mountain heights.

Words to Remember: *Why are you downcast, O my soul? Why so disturbed within me? Put your hope in God, for I will yet praise him, my Savior and my God* (Psalm 42:5-6).

Seven days without prayer makes one weak.

—Allen E. Bartlett

Luke 11

⁵Then he said to them, "Suppose one of you has a friend, and he goes to him at midnight and says, 'Friend, lend me three loaves of bread, ⁶because a friend of mine on a journey has come to me, and I have nothing to set before him.'

⁷"Then the one inside answers, 'Don't bother me. The door is already locked, and my children are with me in bed. I can't get up and give you anything.' ⁸I tell you, though he will not get up and give him the bread because he is his friend, yet because of the man's boldness he will get up and give him as much as he needs.

⁹"So I say to you: Ask and it will be given to you; seek and you will find; knock and the door will be opened to you. ¹⁰For everyone who asks receives; he who seeks finds; and to him who knocks, the door will be opened.

¹¹"Which of you fathers, if your son asks for a fish, will give him a snake instead? ¹²Or if he asks for an egg, will give him a scorpion? ¹³If you then, though you are evil, know how to give good gifts to your children, how much more will your Father in heaven give the Holy Spirit to those who ask him!"

Matthew 15

²¹Leaving that place, Jesus withdrew to the region of Tyre and Sidon. ²²A Canaanite woman from that vicinity came to him, crying out, "Lord, Son of David, have mercy on me! My daughter is suffering terribly from demon-possession."

²³Jesus did not answer a word. So his disciples came to him and urged him, "Send her away, for she keeps crying out after us."

²⁴He answered, "I was sent only to the lost sheep of Israel."

²⁵The woman came and knelt before him. "Lord, help me!" she said.

²⁶He replied, "It is not right to take the children's bread and toss it to their dogs."

²⁷"Yes, Lord," she said, "but even the dogs eat the crumbs that fall from their masters' table."

²⁸Then Jesus answered, "Woman, you have great faith! Your request is granted." And her daughter was healed from that very hour.

CHAPTER 12

Keep on Praying

THIS CHAPTER'S encouraging title raises an intriguing question. What does it mean to "keep on praying"? Does that mean we should make pests of ourselves to God? Should we keep bringing the same requests to Him over and over until He reaches a point of exasperation with us? Does that mean we beg God so long that He finally gives us whatever we want?

"Keep on praying." Does that mean we should pray all the time? Does it mean we should pray as close to 24 hours a day as possible, even if that means neglecting other important duties?

"Keep on praying." Does that mean we should learn to never give up praying though we receive no immediate answers? Do we need to learn to be patient and wait for His timing, without giving up on prayer?

"Keep on praying." We need to learn what that means. We need to understand what Jesus shows us by His teaching and by His example. We need to know so we can learn to exercise faithfulness in prayer. We need to be encouraged and motivated to pray. In this chapter, we explore an encouraging word about prayer—that faithfulness and patience are necessary parts of prayer and are in accord with trusting our loving Heavenly Father.

First, we look at a story of Jesus as it is recorded in Luke's Gospel. In this passage, Jesus used a parable as a teaching device on prayer, just after giving His disciples His model prayer, which we know as the Lord's Prayer. A parable is a short story, based on real-life situations, which is used to illustrate a moral or truth.

Here, Jesus taught about a persistent friend who was rewarded for his tenacity. He used this as an example to encourage all of us to do three things in prayer—ask, seek, and knock. Jesus promised that those who ask, seek, and knock would receive, find, and have doors opened to them. Jesus further taught in the parable under discussion that God's desire to give us our requests far outweighs the desire of even the kindest of our earthly friends.

Also in this chapter, we look at an incident of patient faith that is recorded in Matthew's Gospel. We travel with Jesus out of Israel to the region of Tyre and Sidon along the coast of the Mediterranean Sea. There, Jesus encountered a Canaanite woman. Though Jesus seemed ready to send the woman away because her request did not fit His immediate mission, her patience and understanding of faith helped enable her request to be granted.

Persistence Pays Off

As we explore the practice of prayer, it doesn't take too long before we discover the challenge of perseverance. God calls us to pray, and we know He hears our prayers. Sometimes He answers us in a timely manner. At other times, however, His response is delayed. How shall we pray then? Do we need to keep praying until we get His attention? Do we need to keep praying until we persuade Him that our request is worthy? Having made our request, should we stop praying? Does our persistence reflect a lack of faith? What is the proper understanding of persistence in prayer?

Jesus gave us two pictures of persistence in Luke 11. Both teach us that persistence pays off. They also help us to understand how we can be confidently persistent in prayer. Let's see how they can help us learn to "keep on praying."

Persistence and the Night Visitor

Luke 11:5-13 tells a story that seems strange to us but would have been a familiar and common experience to Jesus' hearers. Jesus told a story about hospitality. It was told to help us understand how to pray.

Jesus' host found himself with a guest who had just arrived at his door late at night. He, in turn, went to a friend to borrow bread so that he could entertain his late visitor.

We would be surprised (and probably a little offended) to have a guest show up at our door in the middle of the night. In the Near East, however, travel might often be delayed until the evening in order to avoid the heat of the sun. The cooler evening temperatures would make travel more bearable. Since travel was slow, often by foot, travelers might not arrive at a destination until late in the night. Since they didn't have phones to call ahead, their host might not know if or when they were coming. You can imagine heads nodding in recognition as Jesus described the situation of the host. "Yes," they seem to say, "that has happened to me."

Once a guest knocked on the door, the rules of hospitality came into play. Today, we might show our unexpected guest a bed and say we would see him or her in the morning. Oriental courtesy, however, called for a generous meal of welcome, so not having food would be a problem. Without refrigerators or preservatives, bread was baked fresh daily. Unless one had overestimated the day's need, no bread would be left at the end of the day. There were no 24-hour grocery stores, so the only other option would be to go ask a friend for some left-over bread. Faced with an embarrassing lack of food, the host in Jesus' parable did just that.

Bringing this need to a friend is the illustration Jesus used to teach us about prayer. The problem was a closed door. In Jesus' culture, a closed door was a definite "Do Not Disturb" sign. During the day, the door would remain open. A closed door in the evening meant the resident had retired for the night.

To call the friend to the door was not only a breach of etiquette; it was a serious inconvenience. The family would be gathered together on the floor. The parents would be at the center, and the children snuggled around them. For the father to rise meant that the whole family would be awakened and disturbed. You can imagine the uproar that could create! It is no wonder that the friend called out, saying he couldn't come to the door and didn't want to be bothered. Still, Jesus pointed out, the man would eventually get up and give his friend the bread to end the disturbance so he could go back to sleep. His motive is not based on his friendship, but on his own self-interest.

How Much More?

The experience of praying can often be an experience of desperate struggle—like Jacob's wrestling with the angel. When Jesus prayed all night, as apparently He often did, we can be sure He was not always simply and quietly waiting before God. One has only to remember Gethsemane to know this. "And being in anguish, he prayed more earnestly, and his sweat was like drops of blood falling to the ground" (Luke 22:44). Or as Hebrews 5:7 tells us, "During the days of Jesus' life on earth, he offered up prayers and petitions with loud cries and tears."

Yet the struggle in prayer is not with God but with us. We speak many words, or the same words over and over again, not because they are needed to persuade God, but because we are often seeking to overcome our own pride, selfishness, or indifference. The struggle in prayer, then, is not our struggle with God but God's struggle with us. It is His hand that will not let us go.

It is important that we do not misunderstand the purpose of Jesus' parable. It is not to provide a model for persistent prayer. The point is not to teach us that we should persist in prayer so that eventually God will answer us just to end the irritation of our asking. Think about the image of God behind that kind of model. It assumes a God who is reluctant to be disturbed by our concerns. It suggests we have to overcome His indifference by annoying Him until He is anxious enough to get rid of us that He grants our request. I certainly hope that is not a true picture of God's attitude toward us!

The story is given, not as a model but to portray contrast. Jesus made the point clear in verses 11-13: "Which of you fathers, if your son asks for a fish, will give him a snake instead? Or if he asks for an egg, will give him a scorpion? If you then, though you are evil, know how to give good gifts to your children, how much more will your Father in heaven give the Holy Spirit to those who ask him!"

If a human neighbor will give a favorable hearing to our need for no better reason than his own self-interest, how much more can we expect from our Heavenly Father! Behind prayer's door we have a God who is already wide-awake, attentive to our call, and responsive to our concern. We don't have to win His interest or attract His attention. If we can experience positive answers to our requests and needs from other people, shouldn't we expect much more from God?

Persistence as Faith in Action

The lesson about prayer that Luke 11 teaches us is about confidence in God's response. It is not about method. It is not even about the virtue of persistence. It is about the goodness we can expect from the One to whom we pray. When we knock on prayer's door, we know that the Master is there for us. He is more anxious to be at work for our good than we are. He already has our interests at heart.

Persistence in prayer is not about changing God's attitude toward us. It is not about gaining His attention. Persistence should be an exercise of faith in action. It is about presenting our concerns and needs in the confidence that the One who hears really cares. It involves continuing to trust and believe even when the prayers don't seem to be answered. We continue to bring those matters to God because we know He cares and because we know we can trust Him.

It is that kind of faith that moved the Canaanite woman in

Matthew 15:21-28. It was her confidence in Jesus that resulted in her request being granted.

I have to admit that this is one story that is a little hard to understand. It is hard to picture Jesus using the image of a dog to illustrate this woman's status. To call a person a dog was a terrible insult. In those days, the dogs were the unclean scavengers of the street.

However, there are two things to remember in this story. First, the tone and the look used when something is said make all the difference in our understanding. Even a phrase that seems mean can be said with a disarming smile. We can call a friend "an old rascal," with a smile and a tone that takes the sting out of it and fills it with affection. We can be relatively sure that the smile on Jesus' face and the compassion in His eyes robbed the words of its insult.

Second, the word used here is not the same word used for the street dogs. Rather, these dogs were little household pets, very different from the vicious dogs that roamed the streets and probed the refuse heaps.

Though Jesus used a form of address that suggests a special household pet, the discussion about the affectionate or familiar tone to the word He used doesn't completely relieve my unease. And that's OK. Scripture shouldn't (and won't) always be "comfortable."

Yet, the heart of the message of this story is clear and positive. This woman came boldly, expressing her specific need directly, out of a faith that was confident in the ability and character of Jesus. She believed that the person "behind the door" would respond to her need. That faith was rewarded, confirming that it had been well founded.

Keep on Praying

If we know that we can expect more from God than our experience with other people, we can pray persistently, knowing that God is waiting to answer our prayers. Our endurance in prayer is sometimes our part in working together with God. Our partnership in tenacity is invited, even called for. It is not our steadfastness, however, that is the basis of our confidence or hope. It is God's gracious intent, His attitude toward us, that is the foundation of our confident faith. "He who did not spare his own Son, but gave him up for us all—how will he not also, along with him, graciously give us all things?" (Romans 8:32).

Even when prayers seem to be unanswered or the answer is delayed, we can be confident that the problem is not God's attitude toward us. He is not unwilling to help us. Sometimes, delay or silence is part of God's best answer to our prayer. There have been times in my life when I became frustrated with God because he didn't give me any answer. Later, I have been able to look back and see that God's silence was His best answer. There were things that needed to happen in me that wouldn't have happened in the right way if I had known the answer. It was God's love and His desire for my best that kept me in the dark. All the time I was pounding on the door, calling for an answer, He was answering.

If God's response is silence, it is not an expression of His indifference but His love. Persistence in prayer is about bringing our needs boldly to God in prayer in the confidence that He is listening. It is grounded in a confidence in God's character and not our persistence. That confidence in God's gracious character and His love for us invites our submissive trust in Him. We can persistently bring the concerns of our hearts to God in prayer, confident that He is listening and responding.

Even when the door remains closed and the house appears to be silent, we can persist at the door because we know He is there for us.

Words to Remember: *So I say to you: Ask and it will be given to you; seek and you will find; knock and the door will be opened to you* (Luke 11:9).

Prayer is exhaling the spirit of man and inhaling the spirit of God. ——Edwin Keith

Psalm 65

[1]Praise awaits you, O God, in Zion;
   to you our vows will be fulfilled.
[2]O you who hear prayer,
   to you all men will come.
[3]When we were overwhelmed by sins,
   you forgave our transgressions.
[4]Blessed are those you choose
   and bring near to live in your courts!
We are filled with the good things of your house,
   of your holy temple.

[5]You answer us with awesome deeds of righteousness,
   O God our Savior,
the hope of all the ends of the earth
   and of the farthest seas,
[6]who formed the mountains by your power,
   having armed yourself with strength,
[7]who stilled the roaring of the seas,
   the roaring of their waves,
   and the turmoil of the nations.
[8]Those living far away fear your wonders;
   where morning dawns and evening fades
   you call forth songs of joy.

[9]You care for the land and water it;
   you enrich it abundantly.
The streams of God are filled with water
   to provide the people with grain,
   for so you have ordained it.
[10]You drench its furrows
   and level its ridges;
you soften it with showers
   and bless its crops.
[11]You crown the year with your bounty,
   and your carts overflow with abundance.
[12]The grasslands of the desert overflow;
   the hills are clothed with gladness.
[13]The meadows are covered with flocks
   and the valleys are mantled with grain;
     they shout for joy and sing.

CHAPTER 13

Thank You, God

As is our normal bedtime routine, my wife and I went in to say good night to our elementary-aged daughter and to pray with her. As we listened to her pray, my wife and I exchanged quick smiles as we heard her oft-repeated requests. "Please, Jesus, help me get a pet puppy—one that is house-broken; and help me have fun tomorrow at school; and help me not to have any nightmares; and help me . . ." My daughter's prayers are very sincere and very appropriate—for her age.

As we mature in our Christian walk, hopefully our prayer lives mature as well. Yet, many adults still find their prayers dominated by an elementary outline of "help me . . ." This chapter encourages us to move to a higher level of communication with God. As we explore Psalm 65, we will be challenged to evaluate the place of thanksgiving in our prayer routines. By elevating the prominence of thanksgiving in our prayers, we move from "what can You do for me?" to "what You have done for me!" language.

God is pleased when we bring our requests before Him. He is even more pleased when we remember to bring our praise and thanksgiving before Him. The psalmist opened the prayer of Psalm 65 with praise and commitment to God. He was grateful that God does not exclude anyone; all persons may come into God's presence. God forgives sins, and that inspired thankfulness in the psalmist.

Then the writer went on to celebrate and thank God for important things: God calls us to Him and provides our needs. God is present in our lives. God shows goodness toward us. And God performs awesome deeds visible in the created world around us. Psalm 65 is a song of joyful praise. From beginning to end, it is a grateful recital of God's works and their benefits. Such songs of joy should be our thankful response as well.

If we as Christians are to be renewed today, we must recover the psalmist's cosmic, comprehensive sense of God, which now we find in Jesus. As Paul put it, "For by him all things were created: things in heaven and on earth, visible and invisible, whether thrones or powers or rulers or authorities; all things were created by him and for him. He is before all things, and in him all things hold together" (Colossians 1:16-17).

Prayer begins when we realize that God exists, is doing good things in this world, and wants to be in relationship with us. That is gratitude, though in a small way, because it is a beginning recognition of who God is. Throughout this book, we have come to a wider and more complete understanding of the meaning and practice of prayer. So, we end as we began but in greater measure—with a psalm of thanksgiving stirring shouts of joy within our hearts.

A Perspective for Prayer

In previous chapters, we have been discovering that prayer is a many-splendored thing. It is a precious experience, a promising opportunity, a sacred burden, and a spiritual mystery. Learning to understand prayer and learning how to pray involve a lifelong journey. We may not always know how to pray or what to pray. However, we want to explore a perspective for prayer that is sure to keep us in focus.

The perspective for prayer that we want to discover is thanksgiving. We can't get very far off-course if we maintain an attitude of gratitude. Thanksgiving need not be limited to a specific response for a specific blessing. We often envision thanksgiving in prayer like we celebrate the holiday of Thanksgiving in the United States—a once-a-year reminder of blessings for which we ought to express thanks. We certainly should practice that kind of gratitude, but the biblical perspective of giving thanks is much more. Thanksgiving should be an attitude and a faith perspective that becomes a lens through which we constantly view our lives and the prayers that we bring to God.

A Point of View for Thanksgiving

Psalm 65 offers us a window into the discovery of thanksgiving in the life of the psalmist and invites us into an experience of its possibilities. Like many psalms, it emerges from the full range of human experience. The psalms are about where we live. There is no shallow sentimentality or superficial spirituality in them. These songs are the fruit of hearts wrestling with life in all its dimensions and finding hope in God in the midst of it all. Thanksgiving doesn't need to begin by pretending that life is always good or easy. Instead, this thanksgiving is with both eyes open, seeing the world just the way it is. The good news is that an attitude of thanksgiving doesn't depend on everything going just right. It can handle the hard side of life too.

Psalm 65 also gives us a perspective for looking forward as well as backward. The translation of this psalm poses some interesting challenges. The opening phrase can be understood to mean that praise is due to God for what He has already done. It can also mean that praise is being offered in the silence before God does what we anticipate that He will do. Many of the statements of God's action in this psalm should be understood as actions begun but not yet completed. This ambiguity may trouble biblical scholars, but it actually helps us. It suggests that the perspective expressed in the psalm includes what God has done *and* what He hasn't done yet. It proposes that thanksgiving is appropriate in the aftermath of God's blessing and in the silence of the anticipation of God's blessing. Thanksgiving brings perspective in both directions.

A Foundation of Faith

The psalmist began his celebration of thanksgiving with an affirmation of faith (vv. 2-4). He made his position clear. He had chosen to place his trust and confidence in God alone. He declared that his past blessings were from God. He also stated his trust in God for his future welfare. "I have cast my lot," he says in effect, "with this God. I will trust Him for my salvation and with my life."

Thanksgiving comes best from such a committed heart. Thanksgiving that is only the result of things having gone well is a weak and temporary attitude. A committed heart can express thanks and confident trust even when circumstances are against us. We can say, "Though he slay me, yet will I hope in him" (Job 13:15). We can look into the "lions' den," the "fiery furnace," or the face of the imperial executioner and still say, "Praise God, from whom all blessings flow."

Faith is the foundation of our thanksgiving. It produces a confident trust. Circumstances may be difficult, but our welfare is entrusted to the One who is beyond circumstances. We know that He has and will care for us. We believe that He is at work for our best. Because that is true, we can be thankful.

Our God Is an Awesome God

The psalmist's faith was not rooted in blind trust alone. He remembered and celebrated the kind of God he trusted:

You answer us with awesome deeds of righteousness,
   O God our Savior,
the hope of all the ends of the earth
   and of the farthest seas,
who formed the mountains by your power,
   having armed yourself with strength,
who stilled the roaring of the seas,
   the roaring of their waves,
   and the turmoil of the nations.
Those living far away fear your wonders;
   where morning dawns and evening fades
      you call forth songs of joy (vv. 5-8).

All of creation declares God's glory and power. The majesty of the mountains only reflects the majesty of the Creator. The awesome power of the sea is only a shadow of the One who masters the sea. The witness of His glory and power extends as far as the dawning of the sun and its setting. "Those living far away" watch with awe as the dawn and sunset shout for joy! Our God is truly an awesome God!

Creation is God's handiwork. We see Him reflected in it. Because that is so, we should have a deep appreciation for nature. Our attitude toward the environment takes on spiritual implications. This is our Father's world. We see Him everywhere in it. He has entrusted this wonder of His creation to us. We will want to honor Him by caring attentively for this gift.

The witness of God's work in creation extends beyond the evidence of His power. It also demonstrates His love and care for us. God could have chosen not to create the world at all. Or He could have created a merely functional world. Such a world would not have required the beauty of color. Everything could have been shades of gray. Pleasant sounds would not be necessary. Food didn't have to taste good. Smells didn't have to be pleasing. The panoramas of the dawn or setting sun are more than necessary. The beauty of the bird's song or of music is more than required.

Pleasant smells and tastes are extras. Every demonstration of beauty in creation beyond necessity is a display of the Creator's extravagance. They are reminders of His love and attentive care for us. This God is truly awesome, and He is *our* God.

The word picture the psalmist used to describe God's blessings was the rainfall after a drought. This scene of abundance and life energized his thanksgiving. No picture could be more powerful in the Near East, where water is such a precious, life-giving commodity. We take water for granted. We feel infringed upon when we can't water our lawns or wash our cars because of a water shortage. The role of water for the psalmist and his peers was much more basic. Water was life. The absence of water meant death. Drought was a serious threat to life and property.

Showers of Blessing

It is the picture of showers of rain pouring out on a dry land that expresses the psalmist's understanding (and expectation) of God's blessings.

You care for the land and water it;
*   you enrich it abundantly.*
The streams of God are filled with water
*   to provide the people with grain . . .*
You drench its furrows
*   and level its ridges;*
you soften it with showers
*   and bless its crops* (vv. 9-10).

These are not meager showers. The water is given in abundance. The streams are filled. The furrows of the fields are drenched. The resulting harvest is rich as God "crowns the year with [His] bounty" (v. 11). The carts that haul the crops away are filled to overflowing, leaving a trail of the rich harvest behind. The hills, meadows, and valleys also reflect the life-giving blessing of God, poured out in abundance. God's goodness finds expression all around us.

The thanksgiving of the psalm communicates a view of God as a giver of blessings in abundance. He doesn't just dole them out cautiously. He lavishes His blessings on His children. The image of God as a generous giver prompted the enthusiastic praise of the psalmist. This generous God, who is anxious to give in abundance, was *his* God.

The character of the language reminds us that the enthusiastic thanksgiving of the psalmist looks in both directions. It is a spontaneous response to blessings received, a drought ended in spectacular fashion. It is also a deep expression of trusting faith. It waits in the silence of the drought and responds with praise. Before a rain cloud begins to appear, the psalmist is able to express thanksgiving. The ground may be dry, but his God is good, faithful, and awesome in His power and generosity. The vision of what God can be expected to do fills the psalmist's heart with a symphony of praise, even in the silence of the drought.

Thank You, God!

The psalmist models a perspective for prayer that is grounded in thanksgiving. It is rooted in his understanding of the God to whom he prayed—the One he trusted. That understanding allowed thanksgiving to shape his prayers. It freed him to give thanks, even when circumstances didn't seem to merit it. Regardless of circumstances, his God, who is greater than circumstances, merited thanksgiving. Such praise gave him a perspective that saw God's blessings and power all around him. Creation became a gift to be honored and treasured as an expression of God's power and love.

We, too, can ground our prayer in thanksgiving. We can respond with gratitude to what God has already done. We can gives thanks in confident faith for what God will do in the future. Thanksgiving brings us into a perspective that lifts and empowers us because it lifts our focus to God. When we pray, thanksgiving is always the right perspective. Even when we are not sure what to pray or how to pray, we can always pray with confident assurance, "Thank You, God!"

Words to Remember: *Be joyful always; pray continually; give thanks in all circumstances, for this is God's will for you in Christ Jesus* (1 Thessalonians 5:16-18).